All's Well That Ends Well

SHAKESPEARE FOR KIDS

JEANETTE VIGON

Copyright © 2023 Jeanette Vigon
All rights reserved.
ISBN: 9798337830810

This book is a modern adaptation for children of William Shakespeare's "All's Well That Ends Well," which is a work in the public domain. While the original story and characters are based on Shakespeare's play, this adaptation includes significant original content tailored for a young audience. These additions include simplified language and reimagined scenes, specifically created to make this timeless tale accessible and engaging for young readers. The intention of this adaptation is to introduce children to the classic story in a manner that respects the essence of Shakespeare's original work, while presenting it in a way that is relatable and understandable for a younger audience.

"We can say of Shakespeare, that never has a man turned so little knowledge to such great account."

— T. S. ELIOT

Why I Wrote This Book The Way I Did

When I embarked on the journey of adapting Shakespeare's plays for children, my primary goal was to bridge the gap between the timeless allure of Shakespeare's narratives and the imaginative worlds of young readers. The decision to adapt these plays for children was driven by a desire to introduce them to the richness of literary classics at an early age, fostering a love for literature that could grow with them.

Choosing to maintain the original structure of acts and scenes was a deliberate effort to preserve the integrity and rhythm of Shakespeare's works. This approach not only honors the original compositions but also introduces young readers to the conventions of drama and the beauty of structured storytelling. It was important to me that children experience the plays as they were intended, albeit in a more accessible form.

Incorporating literary language while ensuring it remains engaging and understandable for children was a balancing act. I aimed to simplify the complexity of Shakespeare's language without diluting its power and beauty. By carefully selecting vocabulary and crafting sentences that convey the essence of the original plays, I aspired to captivate young minds and stimulate their intellectual curiosity.

Adapting these plays also involved making thoughtful choices about content, ensuring that themes and scenes were appropriate for a young audience. This required a sensitive approach to storytelling, where the lessons of love, loyalty, betrayal, and justice are presented in a manner that is both educational and entertaining.

In summary, the creation of this book was a labor of love, guided by the belief that Shakespeare's works are not just for adults but for everyone. By adapting these plays for children, I hope to plant the seeds of appreciation for classic literature in the fertile ground of young imaginations, encouraging a lifelong journey of reading, learning, and discovery.

I truly hope you will enjoy reading it, as much as I enjoyed re-writing it.

A Note for Parents

Dear Parents and Guardians,

Thank you for choosing "All's Well That Ends Well: Shakespeare for Kids." This adaptation is designed to introduce young readers to Shakespeare's rich stories in a way that is both engaging and suitable for children.

Important Note:

Shakespeare's original play, "All's Well That Ends Well," contains themes that may be challenging for young audiences, including issues of deceit, unrequited love, and the complexities of marriage. These themes have been carefully adapted, simplified, or omitted in this version to ensure that the story remains appropriate and enjoyable for children.

The focus of this retelling is on the themes of perseverance, cleverness, and the value of kindness.

In the original play, certain actions and decisions by characters, such as Helena's pursuit of Bertram and the complex dynamics of their relationship, have been reinterpreted to better suit a younger audience. This adaptation emphasizes the importance of determination and resourcefulness, while presenting the story's conflicts and resolutions in a manner that is easy for children to understand and relate to.

Parental Guidance Suggested:

While this adaptation is crafted to be child-friendly, some of the original play's themes and conflicts are inherent to the story and may prompt questions. We encourage parents and guardians to read along with their children and engage in discussions about the characters' choices and the story's lessons. These conversations can enrich your child's understanding and help them develop critical thinking skills while fostering a love for classic literature.

This book is intended as an accessible entry point into Shakespeare's works for young readers. By guiding your child through this adaptation, you can help nurture an early appreciation for the timeless stories and lessons found in Shakespeare's plays.

I hope that you and your children enjoy this retelling of Helena's cleverness and determination, and that it sparks meaningful conversations and a lasting interest in literature.

Thank you for your involvement in your child's reading journey. Your support is invaluable and greatly appreciated.

INTRODUCTION

Welcome to the intriguing and multifaceted world of "All's Well That Ends Well," where the realms of love, ambition, and moral complexity intertwine in a story that is as captivating as it is thought-provoking. This is not just a romantic tale; it is a profound exploration of human desires, the pursuit of happiness, and the complexities of social hierarchy.

Our journey takes us to the courts of France and the rustic fields of Roussillon, where the destinies of our characters are shaped by love, cunning, and the pursuit of what is just and right. In these contrasting settings, we find a diverse cast of characters, each grappling with their own aspirations and ethical dilemmas.

INTRODUCTION

At the center of our tale is Helena, the resourceful and determined daughter of a deceased physician, who is in love with the noble but indifferent Bertram. Despite her lower status, Helena's intelligence and determination set the stage for a story that challenges the norms of social class and the expectations of love.

When Bertram, unwilling to marry Helena despite the king's command, flees to war, Helena devises a bold and clever plan to win his love and respect. Along the way, she navigates a world where virtue is tested, loyalty is questioned, and the true meaning of "all's well that ends well" is explored through her actions and the responses of those around her.

But this story is far from a simple love conquest—it delves into the intricacies of human motivation, the power dynamics within relationships, and the moral ambiguity that often accompanies the pursuit of personal goals. Fear not, though, for within the twists of deception and the challenges of unrequited love, we find moments of humor, wisdom, and the enduring belief in the power of determination and virtue.

We will celebrate Helena's wit and perseverance, admire the wisdom of the older generation, and question the actions of those who seek only their own advancement. Through their journeys, we'll uncover lessons about the nature of love, the

INTRODUCTION

importance of honesty, and the ultimate triumph of good intentions over adversity.

So, prepare yourself for a story that is both a reflection on the nature of love and a critique of societal norms. Imagine scenes filled with clever disguises, heartfelt confessions, and the trials that come with testing the boundaries of what is right and what is merely convenient. In this tale, love is a game of wits, virtue is a guiding force, and the outcome is a testament to the power of persistence.

Are you ready to dive into this world where love, ambition, and moral quandaries collide? Then let's begin our adventure with Helena, Bertram, and the colorful cast of characters who will teach us that, in the end, it is not just about winning but about winning with integrity and heart. Welcome to "All's Well That Ends Well," where every choice leads us closer to understanding the true meaning of love, virtue, and the ultimate quest for a life well-lived!

ACT 1

SCENE I

In the grand halls of the Count's palace in Rousillon, the air was heavy with sadness. Bertram, a young lord, stood beside his mother, the Countess. They were both dressed in black, mourning the recent loss of Bertram's father. Helena, a kind and gentle young woman, and Lafeu, a wise and older lord, were also present.

The Countess sighed deeply, her voice filled with sorrow. "As I send my son away, it feels like I'm losing my husband all over again."

Bertram, with tears in his eyes, responded, "And as I leave,

Mother, I grieve for Father once more. But I must follow the king's command. Now, I belong to him, and I must obey."

Lafeu, trying to comfort them, said, "Madam, you'll find a father in the king, and you, young sir, will find a new protector. The king is a good man, and he will surely show you the same kindness your father would have."

The Countess, worried, asked, "Is there any hope that the king will get better?"

Lafeu shook his head sadly. "He has given up on his doctors, madam. They've tried everything, but all they've managed to do is lose hope over time."

The Countess turned to Helena, who had been quietly listening. "This young woman's father was a doctor, a very skilled and honest man. If his knowledge could have gone beyond the limits of nature, he would have defeated death itself. If only he were alive today, I believe he could cure the king."

. . .

Lafeu was curious. "What was his name, madam?"

The Countess replied, "He was a well-known and respected man—Gerard de Narbon."

Lafeu nodded, remembering. "Indeed, he was exceptional. The king spoke of him recently, with great admiration and sorrow. If anyone's knowledge could defy mortality, it would have been his."

Bertram asked, "What illness does the king suffer from?"

Lafeu answered, "A serious one, my lord, called a fistula."

Bertram was surprised. "I hadn't heard about this before."

Lafeu sighed. "I wish it were less well-known. Was this young woman the daughter of Gerard de Narbon?"

. . .

The Countess smiled warmly at Helena. "Yes, she is his only child. She has been under my care, and I have high hopes for her. She is as good as her upbringing suggests, and she has inherited her father's qualities. Her virtues are simple and pure, making her all the more admirable."

Lafeu noticed tears in Helena's eyes. "Madam, your praises are bringing her to tears."

The Countess gently said to Helena, "These tears are the best way for a maiden to honor her virtues. But Helena, no more tears. If you continue, people will think you are pretending to be sad."

Helena softly replied, "I truly feel sorrow, but I am also pretending to be strong."

Lafeu offered some advice. "Moderate grief is proper for the dead, but too much sorrow can harm the living."

The Countess added, "If the living resist grief, then too much sadness can even be dangerous."

. . .

Bertram, ready to leave, asked his mother, "Madam, please give me your blessings."

Lafeu, puzzled, asked, "What do you mean by that?"

The Countess blessed her son, "May you be blessed, Bertram, and may you take after your father in both character and appearance. Let your blood and virtue guide you, and let goodness be your birthright. Love everyone, trust a few, and do wrong to no one. Be strong enough for your enemies but use your power wisely. Keep your friends close and speak wisely. May heaven give you all you need, and may my prayers help you. Farewell, my son. Lafeu, please guide him."

Lafeu assured her, "He won't lack for anything, madam. He will be well cared for."

The Countess whispered a final blessing, "Heaven bless him. Farewell, Bertram."

. . .

As Bertram prepared to leave, he turned to Helena and said, "I wish you the best, Helena. Take care of my mother, and make sure she's well looked after."

Lafeu also bid farewell, "Farewell, dear lady. Uphold your father's honor."

As Bertram and Lafeu departed, Helena was left alone. Her heart ached not just for her father but also for Bertram. She sighed, "Oh, if only that were all! I hardly think of my father now. My tears for him are nothing compared to those I shed for Bertram. What was my father like? I've almost forgotten him. My thoughts are filled only with Bertram. I can't live without him. Loving him feels as impossible as trying to reach a star in the sky. He is so far above me, like a star shining brightly. My love for him brings me pain. How foolish I am to love someone so far out of my reach! But I loved seeing him every hour, imagining his handsome face in my mind. But now he's gone, and all I have left are memories. Who's coming now?"

Helena noticed Parolles, a bold and talkative soldier, entering. She thought to herself, "Here comes one of Bertram's friends. I like him because he is close to Bertram, though I know he talks too much and often exaggerates. Still, he is part of Bertram's world, so I tolerate him."

Parolles greeted Helena with a cheerful smile. "Greetings, fair lady!"

Helena smiled back, playing along. "And to you, brave soldier!"

Parolles noticed Helena seemed thoughtful and asked, "What are you thinking about?"

Helena replied, "I was just thinking about how difficult it can be to protect the things we care about."

Parolles, always ready with an answer, said, "The best way to protect something is to be strong and smart. If you're clever, you can outwit any challenge that comes your way."

Helena nodded, "But what if the challenge is too great, and we feel too small to face it?"

. . .

Parolles, trying to sound wise, said, "Sometimes, when a challenge is too big, it's okay to ask for help. Friends and allies can make even the toughest problems easier to handle."

Helena smiled, feeling a little more at ease. "That's good advice, Parolles. It's important to have good friends."

Parolles grinned, pleased with himself. "Indeed it is! And you, dear Helena, are a good friend to many. Don't worry too much about challenges; just remember to stay strong and keep your friends close."

Just then, a page entered and informed Parolles that Bertram was calling for him. Parolles bid farewell to Helena, saying, "Goodbye, Helena. If I remember you, I will think of you at court."

Helena smiled warmly. "Thank you, Parolles. I hope you have a safe journey."

. . .

Parolles, feeling proud, said, "And you, Helena, stay hopeful and strong. Farewell!"

After he left, Helena thought to herself, "Sometimes, we think our problems are bigger than they really are. But if we believe in ourselves and keep our friends close, we can find the strength to face anything. I just need to be brave and true to myself, and maybe things will work out." And with that, Helena left, her heart filled with hope and determination.

SCENE 2

In the grand and majestic halls of the King's palace in Paris, trumpets sounded, announcing the arrival of the King of France. He entered, holding letters, surrounded by several attendants. The King's expression was serious as he began to speak.

"The Florentines and Senoys are at war with each other," the King said, "They've fought with equal strength and continue their fierce battle."

One of the lords present nodded. "So it's reported, sir."

. . .

The King continued, "Indeed, it's confirmed. We've received word from our cousin in Austria, who warns that the Florentines may soon ask for our help. Our dearest ally, however, suggests that we refuse."

The first lord, understanding the situation, added, "His love and wisdom, trusted by your majesty, should be enough reason to take his advice seriously."

The King sighed. "He has already prepared our response, denying Florence's request even before they've made it. Yet, for the young men here who wish to see the Tuscan service, they have permission to join whichever side they choose."

Another lord spoke up. "It might serve as good experience for our young nobles, who are eager for adventure and action."

Just then, the King noticed new arrivals. "Who comes here?" he asked.

The first lord recognized them immediately. "It is the Count of Rousillon, my good lord, young Bertram."

. . .

The King looked at Bertram with a thoughtful gaze. "Youth, you carry your father's face. Nature, with great care, has shaped you well. May you inherit your father's virtues too! Welcome to Paris."

Bertram bowed respectfully. "My thanks and duty are to your majesty."

The King, reminiscing about the past, said, "I wish I had the same strength now as when your father and I first served together. He was a brave man, one of the best. He lasted long in the service, but old age eventually caught up with both of us, wearing us out. It brings me comfort to speak of your good father. In his youth, he had the same wit I see in our young lords today, though they often jest too much and forget the importance of honor. Your father, however, was different. He was a true courtier, never bitter or contemptuous. He knew exactly when to speak and when to remain silent, always treating those below him with respect, making them proud to know him. He was a man that these younger lords could learn from."

. . .

Bertram listened with admiration. "Your memories of him, sir, are richer than any words on his tombstone. His true legacy lives in your speech."

The King, lost in his thoughts, said wistfully, "I wish I could be with him again. He had a way of speaking that stayed with you, planting wisdom in your mind. I can almost hear him now, saying, 'Let me not live beyond my time, when my flame burns low, to become nothing more than a memory to younger spirits who only care for new things.' He wished not to outlive his usefulness, and I share that wish now. Since I can no longer bring anything new, I feel it's time to step aside."

Another lord, noticing the King's somber mood, tried to comfort him. "You are loved, sir. Even those who take your presence for granted will miss you first when you're gone."

The King nodded, acknowledging the truth. "I know I still have a place here. How long has it been, Count, since your father's physician passed away? He was much respected."

Bertram answered, "It's been about six months, my lord."

. . .

The King sighed. "If he were still alive, I would seek his help. Lend me your arm; the others have worn me out with their various treatments. Nature and sickness will take their time to decide the outcome. Welcome, Count. You are as dear to me as my own son."

Bertram bowed again, grateful. "Thank you, your majesty."

With that, the King and his attendants departed, leaving Bertram to reflect on the honor and responsibility now resting on his young shoulders.

SCENE 3

In the Count's palace in Rousillon, the Countess entered the room with her Steward and a cheerful servant, often called the Clown.

The Countess turned to the Steward. "What do you have to say about this young woman?"

The Steward, wanting to be respectful, replied, "Madam, I've always tried to please you in every way. I hope my efforts show that, but I don't want to brag too much about my own work."

. . .

The Countess then noticed the Clown standing nearby. "What is this rascal doing here? Get out, sir! I've heard complaints about you, and though I don't believe all of them, I know you're certainly capable of causing trouble."

The Clown, pretending to be hurt, said, "Madam, you know I'm just a poor fellow."

The Countess responded with some impatience, "Well, what is it?"

The Clown continued, "No, madam, it's not so well that I'm poor, though some rich folks might end up in trouble too. But if you'll allow it, Isbel and I wish to get married and make our way in the world."

The Countess, surprised, asked, "Do you really want to be a beggar?"

The Clown shrugged, "I'm just asking for your blessing in this."

. . .

The Countess questioned him further, "In what exactly?"

The Clown explained, "In the matter of Isbel and me. Working in service isn't a lifelong promise, and I think I won't be truly blessed until I have a family of my own. People say children are blessings, after all."

Curious, the Countess asked, "Why do you want to get married?"

The Clown, with a playful grin, replied, "Madam, my heart longs for it. Sometimes, we're driven by our feelings, and I believe it's the right thing to do."

The Countess asked skeptically, "Is that your only reason?"

The Clown, trying to sound wise, said, "I have other reasons too, though they might not be as noble."

The Countess, still doubtful, asked, "Would you share them?"

. . .

The Clown chuckled, "Madam, I've made my share of mistakes, like everyone else. But I want to marry so that I can start fresh and be a better person."

The Countess sighed, "Your marriage might come sooner than your repentance."

The Clown admitted, "I'm low on friends right now, but I hope to gain some through my wife."

The Countess warned, "The kind of friends you gain that way might be your enemies, fool."

The Clown, not taking her seriously, replied, "Madam, even those who might seem like enemies can sometimes help us in ways we don't expect."

Growing tired of his antics, the Countess asked, "Will you always be such a troublesome fool?"

. . .

The Clown responded with a rhyme, "Madam, I'm just telling it as I see it. 'Marriage comes by fate, and the rest we take as it is.'"

The Countess, finally having enough, said, "Go on now, and do as I asked."

The Steward then spoke up, "Madam, shall I ask Helena to come to you? She's the one I need to speak about."

The Countess agreed, "Yes, go tell Helena I wish to speak with her."

The Clown, in his usual manner, began to sing a silly song as he left the room, "Was this fair face the cause of all the trouble? Oh, what a pity, oh, what a joy."

The Countess interrupted him, "What's that song you're butchering now, fool?"

. . .

The Clown replied, "It's a song about finding one good person among many, madam. If only the world could be so lucky all the time."

The Countess, growing exasperated, said, "Go on, get out of here, and do as I said."

The Clown, still talking to himself, said, "Ah, that a man should be at a woman's command and yet no harm done! I'm going, madam, to fetch Helena."

Once the Clown had left, the Countess turned to the Steward. "Well?"

The Steward began, "Madam, I know you care deeply for Helena."

The Countess nodded, "Yes, I do. Her father entrusted her to me, and she deserves all the love I can give her. She's owed much more than she asks for, and I intend to give her what she needs."

. . .

The Steward continued, "Madam, I was near her recently, closer than she might have wished. She was alone, speaking her thoughts aloud, thinking no one else could hear. She spoke of how she loves your son. She felt it was unfair that fortune has placed them in such different positions. She believes that love should not be hindered by status, and she was deeply sorrowful about it. I thought it my duty to inform you, as this concerns you."

The Countess, reflecting on his words, said, "You've done well to tell me. I had suspected something like this before, but I wasn't sure. Leave me now, and keep this to yourself. I'll speak with you more about this later."

The Steward left, and Helena entered the room.

The Countess looked at her with understanding. "When I was young, I felt just as you do now. Love and longing are natural at your age."

Helena, noticing the Countess's serious tone, asked, "What do you wish to say, madam?"

. . .

The Countess gently said, "You know, Helena, I think of you as a daughter."

Helena replied with respect, "You are like a mother to me, madam."

The Countess insisted, "No, Helena, not just like a mother—I *am* your mother. Why do you seem startled when I say that? What's wrong with calling me your mother? I care for you as if you were born to me. Does it upset you to hear that?"

Helena, distressed, responded, "It's not that, madam. It's just that I'm not truly your daughter. Your son, the Count, cannot be my brother. I come from a humble background, and he is of noble birth. He is my master, and I will always serve him faithfully, but he cannot be my brother."

The Countess asked gently, "But could you be my daughter-in-law, then? Does your heart long for my son in that way?"

. . .

Helena, feeling exposed, confessed, "Madam, I do love your son. I love him deeply, though I know it's hopeless. My family was poor, but honest, and so is my love. I don't seek anything from him, nor would I wish to have him until I'm worthy. But I can't help how I feel. I know it's in vain, but I still pour out my love, even though I know it will bring me heartache. Please don't hate me for loving where you do. If you ever felt true love, then I hope you can pity me."

The Countess, now understanding everything, asked, "Did you recently plan to go to Paris?"

Helena admitted, "Yes, madam, I did."

The Countess asked, "Why? Tell me the truth."

Helena, gathering her courage, replied, "I will tell you the truth, madam. My father left me some special remedies that he had discovered through his work. Among them is one that could cure the king of his illness. That was why I wanted to go to Paris."

. . .

The Countess, impressed, asked, "And was this really your reason for going?"

Helena nodded. "Yes, madam, it was. But your son made me think of it. If it weren't for him, I might not have thought about Paris, the medicine, or the king."

The Countess thought for a moment. "But do you think the king would accept your help? He and his doctors have given up hope. How would they trust someone as young and inexperienced as you, when all the learned scholars have failed?"

Helena, with quiet determination, replied, "There's more to it than just my father's skill, madam. I believe that with the help of the stars and some good fortune, I can cure the king. If you would allow me to try, I would gladly risk everything."

The Countess asked, "Do you truly believe this?"

Helena nodded. "Yes, madam, I do."

. . .

The Countess, moved by her sincerity, said, "Then you shall have my permission and my support. I'll provide you with everything you need, and I'll send you off with my blessings. Go to Paris tomorrow, and remember that I'm with you in spirit."

Helena, overwhelmed with gratitude, thanked her. The Countess smiled and reassured her, "Whatever I can do to help you, you shall have."

With that, they both left the room, preparing for the journey ahead.

ACT II

SCENE 1

In the grand palace of the King in Paris, the King was bidding farewell to several young lords who were preparing to leave for the war in Florence. Among them were Bertram and his companion, Parolles. The atmosphere was serious, yet filled with a sense of duty and honor.

The King addressed the young men, "Farewell, young lords. Hold onto the principles of war that you have learned, and use them wisely. Share your wisdom with each other. If you both learn and grow, the reward will be enough for you all."

. . .

One of the lords responded, "It's our hope, sir, that we will return as seasoned soldiers and find you in good health."

The King, however, was not so optimistic. "No, no, I fear my health may not improve, but my heart still fights against admitting how serious my illness is. Farewell, young lords. Whether I live or die, be the sons of worthy Frenchmen. Go to Italy not just to seek honor, but to earn it truly. Let the world see your courage and remember your deeds. I say farewell."

Another lord added, "We wish you good health, Your Majesty!"

The King then offered some advice, "Be cautious of the women in Italy. They say our Frenchmen lack the words to refuse their advances. Beware of being trapped before you've even begun to serve."

Both lords responded, "We will take your warnings to heart."

The King nodded, "Farewell," and exited with his attendants.

. . .

As the lords prepared to leave, one turned to Bertram. "Oh, my sweet lord, will you stay behind?"

Parolles quickly interjected, "It's not his fault; he's being held back."

Another lord said eagerly, "Ah, war is glorious!"

Parolles agreed, "It certainly is. I've seen those wars myself."

Bertram, frustrated, explained, "I've been ordered to stay here, being told I'm 'too young' or 'it's too early' for me to go."

Parolles, always ready with advice, suggested, "If you're determined, boy, slip away and join the war bravely."

Bertram, feeling trapped, replied, "I'll end up just pacing

around here while others earn honor in battle. By heaven, I'll find a way to sneak away."

One lord supported him, "There's honor in that decision."

Parolles encouraged him, "Do it, Count."

Another lord added, "I'll support you too. Farewell."

Bertram felt torn but determined. "I'm with you, and leaving you feels like tearing myself apart."

As the lords bid farewell, Parolles added with a touch of bravado, "Goodbye, noble heroes! Remember to tell Captain Spurio, the one with the scar on his cheek, that I'm alive. Observe how he speaks of me."

The lords promised, "We will, noble captain," and they exited.

. . .

Parolles, left alone with Bertram, mused, "May Mars, the god of war, bless you, young warriors! So, what will you do?"

Bertram replied, "Wait—the King is coming."

Just then, the King re-entered, causing Bertram and Parolles to step back respectfully.

Parolles whispered to Bertram, "Be more gracious in your farewell to the lords. You held back too much. They are the leaders of the time, and even if their actions are sometimes questionable, they are to be followed. Go after them and give a proper farewell."

Bertram agreed, "I will do so," and they both exited.

Shortly after, Lafeu entered, bowing deeply before the King. "Pardon me, my lord, for both myself and the message I bring."

The King, sensing seriousness, said, "Stand up and speak."

. . .

Lafeu stood and said, "There's someone here who might be able to cure your illness. Would you be willing to see her?"

The King, surprised, asked, "Who is this 'her'?"

Lafeu explained, "She's a doctor, my lord. I've spoken with her, and though she's young, she has an impressive knowledge of medicine. She wishes to see you."

The King, intrigued, said, "Bring her in. Let's see what this wonder is all about."

Lafeu exited briefly and returned with Helena.

Lafeu introduced her, "This is his majesty, speak to him as you wish. I'll leave you to it."

Lafeu left, leaving Helena alone with the King.

. . .

The King, looking at Helena, asked, "What brings you here, young lady?"

Helena, gathering her courage, replied, "My lord, my father was Gerard de Narbon, a respected doctor. Before he died, he entrusted me with a special remedy, one he believed could cure the very illness that afflicts you. I come humbly to offer it to you."

The King, though grateful, was skeptical. "We've had the best doctors, and they've all said there's no cure. How can we trust a remedy from someone so young?"

Helena, undeterred, replied, "Sometimes the greatest works are done by the least expected. Miracles have come from humble sources before. Please, let me try."

The King, touched by her sincerity, asked, "What makes you so confident?"

Helena answered, "If within two days you're not better, I'm

willing to face any consequences. But if I succeed, will you grant me one request?"

The King, impressed by her bravery, said, "Make your request, and I promise to grant it."

Helena took a deep breath. "I ask for the right to choose my own husband from among those who serve you."

The King, surprised by the simplicity of her request, agreed. "If you can cure me, you shall have your wish. You have my word."

Helena, grateful, promised, "I will do everything I can to help you."

The King, feeling hopeful for the first time in a long while, said, "Then let's begin. If you succeed, your reward will be great."

And with that, they both left the room.

SCENE 2

In the Count's palace in Rousillon, the Countess entered with the Clown, who was known for his playful and witty remarks.

The Countess, ready to test him, said, "Come on, sir; I'm going to see just how well you've been trained."

The Clown, ever quick with a response, replied, "I will show myself as someone well-fed but simply taught. I know my place is only at court."

. . .

The Countess, curious, asked, "To the court? Why do you speak of it with such disdain? But to the court!"

The Clown explained, "Madam, if a man has any manners at all, he may easily lose them at court. If he can't bow properly, take off his hat, kiss his hand, and say nothing, then he's not fit for court. But as for me, I have an answer that will suit anyone."

The Countess smiled, "Well, that's a generous answer, fitting for all questions."

The Clown continued with a grin, "It's like a barber's chair, madam; it fits everyone, whether they're skinny, plump, or anything in between."

The Countess, amused, asked, "Will your answer really fit all questions?"

The Clown responded with humor, "As perfectly as ten groats fit the hand of a lawyer, or as a French crown suits a fancy dress. My answer is as fitting as a pancake on Shrove Tuesday, a dance on May Day, or a nail in its hole."

The Countess, entertained, asked, "So, you have an answer that fits all questions?"

The Clown boasted, "From the duke down to the constable, my answer will fit any question."

The Countess teased, "It must be a very large answer to fit all demands."

The Clown, still joking, said, "It's actually quite simple, if the truth were told. Here it is, and it includes everything. Ask me if I'm a courtier, and you'll see."

The Countess, indulging him, said, "If only we could be young again. I'll play the fool and hope to learn from your answer. Tell me, sir, are you a courtier?"

. . .

The Clown, with exaggerated politeness, replied, "Oh Lord, madam! There's a simple answer. I could give you a hundred more like it."

The Countess played along, "Sir, I am a humble friend of yours, who cares for you."

The Clown responded with more exaggerated politeness, "Oh Lord, madam! Say as much as you like."

The Countess continued, "I think, sir, that you can't eat this plain food."

The Clown replied, "Oh Lord, madam! Go ahead, I can handle it."

The Countess then said, "I believe you were whipped recently, sir."

The Clown, undeterred, answered, "Oh Lord, madam! Don't hold back."

. . .

The Countess laughed, "Do you cry 'Oh Lord, sir!' when you're whipped, and say 'Don't hold back'? Indeed, your 'Oh Lord, sir!' fits well with a whipping. You'd respond perfectly to one if you were tied to it."

The Clown, with a sigh, said, "I've never had worse luck with my 'Oh Lord, sir!' I guess some things serve well for a time, but not forever."

The Countess, still amused, remarked, "I'm playing the part of a noblewoman by spending time so merrily with a fool."

The Clown, catching the joke, replied, "Oh Lord, madam! See, it serves well again."

The Countess decided it was time to get serious. "Enough, sir; to your business. Give this to Helena, and ask her for an immediate answer. Send my regards to my kinsmen and my son. It's not much."

. . .

The Clown, understanding, said, "Not much praise for them."

The Countess clarified, "Not much work for you. Do you understand?"

The Clown, with a bow, said, "Most certainly. I'm ahead of myself already."

The Countess nodded, "Be quick about it."

With that, they both exited, each going their separate ways.

SCENE 3

In the King's grand palace in Paris, Bertram, Lafeu, and Parolles were deep in conversation. Lafeu, an older and wise man, said, "People say miracles no longer happen, and now we have clever thinkers who explain away things that once seemed magical. We pretend to know everything when we should sometimes just be in awe of the unknown."

Parolles, always eager to agree, added, "Indeed, it's the most wondrous thing that has come about recently."

Bertram, the young nobleman, nodded. "It truly is."

. . .

Lafeu continued, "Even the most skilled doctors gave up on him—"

Parolles quickly interrupted, "Exactly, as I was saying."

Lafeu went on, ignoring Parolles, "Not even the great Galen or Paracelsus could help him."

Parolles repeated, "So I said."

Lafeu mentioned, "All the wise and learned men declared him incurable."

Parolles chimed in again, "That's right; I said the same."

Lafeu sighed and said, "Yes, but now it's clear that a great miracle has taken place, something that goes beyond just healing the King."

Parolles agreed, "I would have said that too."

. . .

Just then, the King entered with Helena and several attendants. Lafeu and Parolles stepped back as the King called for the lords in the court. He invited Helena to sit beside him, praising her for healing his hand, and promised her a great reward.

The lords entered, and the King told Helena, "These young noblemen stand before you. You may choose any one of them as your husband, and they cannot refuse."

Helena, blushing, said, "I wish for each of you to find a fair and virtuous wife when Love wills it. But for now, I must choose just one."

Lafeu, watching the young lords, joked, "If I were younger, I'd be as bold as these boys, with not a worry in the world."

Helena, modest and humble, finally approached Bertram. She said, "I dare not say I take you, but I offer myself and my service to you. I will be yours forever."

. . .

The King, seeing this, said, "Then take her, Bertram; she is your wife."

But Bertram protested, "My lord, I cannot marry her. I beg you to let me choose with my own eyes."

The King was surprised. "Do you not know what she has done for me?"

Bertram replied, "Yes, my lord, but that doesn't mean I should marry her. She was raised in my father's house, and I can't see her as anything but the daughter of a poor doctor. How could I ever marry her?"

The King, growing stern, said, "You only look down on her because of her humble background, but don't you see? Virtue and goodness can come from anywhere, no matter how lowly. She has healed me, and that alone makes her worthy. You are wrong to reject her."

. . .

Bertram stubbornly responded, "I cannot love her, and I won't try to."

The King, now angry, said, "You do yourself a disservice. You should be grateful. Obey me, or I will cast you out of my favor forever."

Realizing the King was serious, Bertram reluctantly said, "I will submit to your will, my lord. I see now that she is worthy because you have made her so."

The King then ordered Bertram to take Helena's hand and said, "Good fortune will smile upon this marriage. We will have a grand ceremony tonight."

After everyone but Lafeu and Parolles left, Lafeu turned to Parolles and said, "Your master was wise to change his mind."

Parolles, shocked, asked, "Change his mind? My lord, my master?"

. . .

Lafeu replied, "Yes, isn't that what I said?"

Parolles grumbled, "You are too old, sir. You speak in riddles."

Lafeu, not bothered, said, "And you are not as clever as you think. I've known you for a while, and now I see you for what you are—good for nothing."

Parolles, angry, muttered, "If you weren't so old—"

But Lafeu cut him off, saying, "Don't get too angry, or you'll regret it. Farewell, my good-for-nothing fellow."

Parolles fumed after Lafeu left, vowing to get back at him somehow.

Bertram soon returned, distressed. "I'm doomed!" he exclaimed. "They've married me off, and I don't want this marriage."

. . .

Parolles, trying to comfort him, said, "Let's go to war, leave France behind. Who cares about this place?"

Bertram agreed, deciding to send Helena back to his house, write to the King, and flee to the wars in Italy.

Parolles, seeing his friend's resolve, urged him on, saying, "Yes, let's leave her behind. The King has done you wrong, but we can fix it."

And with that, they left together, planning their escape.

SCENE 4

In the King's palace in Paris, Helena met with the Clown, who brought her news. Helena asked, "How is my mother? Does she greet me kindly? Is she well?"

The Clown, known for his playful nature, replied, "She is not well, but she still has her health. She's very cheerful, but not well. Thanks be given, she's doing well enough and wants for nothing in the world, but she's not entirely well."

Helena, puzzled, asked, "If she's very well, what ails her that she's not entirely well?"

. . .

The Clown answered, "Truly, she's well indeed, except for two things."

Helena asked, "What two things?"

The Clown, with a mischievous grin, said, "One, that she's not in heaven, where God might send her quickly. And the other, that she's still on earth, from where God might also send her quickly!"

At that moment, Parolles entered, greeting Helena warmly, "Bless you, my fortunate lady!"

Helena responded, "I hope, sir, you wish me well as I follow my own good fortune."

Parolles nodded, "You had my prayers to guide you, and to keep them, you still have them. Oh, my knave, how is my old lady doing?"

. . .

The Clown, always ready with a jest, replied, "If you had her wrinkles and I had her money, I would wish she were as you say."

Parolles, confused, said, "Why, I say nothing."

The Clown continued, "Well, you're the wiser man for it; many a man's tongue leads to his own undoing. To say nothing, do nothing, know nothing, and have nothing—that's almost your entire title, which is very close to nothing."

Parolles, growing irritated, said, "Away with you! You're a knave."

The Clown shot back, "You should have said, 'Before a knave, thou'rt a knave,' meaning 'before me, thou'rt a knave.' That would have been the truth, sir."

Parolles, trying to regain his composure, said, "Go on, you're a witty fool; I've discovered that much."

. . .

The Clown grinned, "Did you find that in yourself, sir? Or were you taught to find it? The search was worthwhile, and you might find much more foolishness within, enough to amuse the world and increase laughter."

Parolles, trying to end the banter, said, "A good knave, indeed, and well-fed."

Turning to Helena, Parolles continued, "Madam, my lord will leave tonight. A very serious matter calls him away. The great privilege and duty of love, which time claims as your right, he acknowledges. But he must delay it, though this delay is filled with sweetness, making the coming time overflow with joy."

Helena, concerned, asked, "What else does he want?"

Parolles answered, "He asks that you take your leave of the King quickly, making it seem like your own decision, supported by whatever explanation you think is necessary."

Helena asked again, "What more does he command?"

. . .

Parolles replied, "Once you have done this, you are to wait for his further instructions."

Helena, ever dutiful, said, "In everything, I will do as he wishes."

Parolles nodded, "I shall report it so."

Helena replied, "Please do."

After Parolles left, Helena turned to the Clown and said, "Come along, sirrah."

And with that, they left the palace together.

SCENE 5

In the King's palace in Paris, Lafeu and Bertram were deep in conversation. Lafeu, with a skeptical tone, said, "But I hope, my lord, you don't truly believe him to be a soldier."

Bertram, defending his friend, replied, "Yes, my lord, I do. He's proven himself to be very brave."

Lafeu, with a hint of doubt, remarked, "You've heard this from his own words, I suppose?"

Bertram nodded. "And from others who vouch for him."

. . .

Lafeu shook his head slightly. "Then perhaps my judgment is off. I thought he was more like a common bird, not the noble one he claims to be."

Bertram reassured him, "I assure you, my lord, he's knowledgeable and courageous."

Lafeu, half-joking, admitted, "Then I must have misjudged him, but I find it hard to regret my error. Here he comes now. Please, help us make peace; I'll do my part to be friendly."

As Parolles approached, he greeted Bertram, "These matters will be taken care of, sir."

Lafeu, with a playful tone, asked Parolles, "Tell me, sir, who is your tailor?"

Parolles, caught off guard, responded, "Sir?"

. . .

Lafeu continued, "Oh, I know him well. He's a skilled craftsman, a very good tailor."

Bertram, wanting to check on something else, whispered to Parolles, "Is she gone to the King?"

Parolles replied, "She is."

Bertram asked, "Will she leave tonight?"

Parolles answered, "As you wish."

Bertram, thinking ahead, said, "I've written my letters, packed my belongings, and arranged for our horses. Tonight, when I should begin my duties as a husband, I'll end it before it starts."

Lafeu, speaking aloud and observing Parolles, said, "A good traveler might have something to offer at the end of a meal, but one who lies and talks endlessly about nothing should be listened to once and then beaten three times. God save you, captain."

Bertram, sensing tension, asked, "Is there some unkindness between you and my lord, monsieur?"

Parolles, confused, replied, "I don't know how I've earned his displeasure."

Lafeu, with a chuckle, said, "You've managed to fall into it, boots and all, like someone jumping into a pie. And you'll run out of it just as quickly to avoid being questioned."

Bertram, trying to smooth things over, suggested, "Perhaps you've misunderstood him, my lord."

Lafeu, with a sigh, replied, "And I will continue to misunderstand him, even if I caught him praying. Farewell, my lord. And believe me, there's nothing of substance in this shallow man. His soul is in his clothes. Don't trust him with anything serious. I've known many like him, and I know their nature. Farewell, monsieur. I've spoken better of you than you deserve, but we must do good even when faced with evil."

As Lafeu exited, Parolles muttered, "What an idle lord. I swear."

Bertram agreed, "I think so too."

Parolles, trying to gauge Bertram's opinion, asked, "Why, don't you know him?"

Bertram replied, "Yes, I know him well, and people speak highly of him. But here comes my burden."

Helena entered, and addressed Bertram, "I've spoken with the King as you commanded and received his permission to leave. However, he wishes to speak with you privately."

Bertram, with a hint of impatience, said, "I will obey his will. Helen, don't be surprised at my actions. They don't seem fitting for the time, nor do they match my duties. I wasn't prepared for such a situation, so I seem unsettled. I must ask you to return home immediately. Please don't question my request too much; my reasons are better than they appear. Here, take this letter to my mother."

He handed her a letter, adding, "It will be two days before I see you again. I leave you to your wisdom."

Helena, feeling resigned, said, "Sir, I have nothing to say except that I am your most obedient servant."

Bertram, brushing off her words, replied, "Come, come, no more of that."

Helena, with a heavy heart, continued, "And I always will be, trying to make up for what my humble fate has lacked compared to my great fortune."

Bertram dismissed her concerns, "Let that go. I'm in a hurry. Farewell; hurry home."

. . .

Helena, seeking his pardon, said, "Please, sir, forgive me."

Bertram, slightly impatient, asked, "Well, what would you say?"

Helena hesitated, then confessed, "I'm not worthy of the good fortune I possess, nor do I dare to claim it as mine, even though it is. But like a timid thief, I almost want to take what is lawfully mine."

Bertram, trying to understand, asked, "What do you want?"

Helena, struggling with her words, replied, "Something, and yet hardly anything. Nothing, really. I don't want to say what I want, my lord. But yes, I should. Strangers and enemies part with a kiss, not with distance."

Bertram, not wanting to linger, said, "I pray you, don't delay. Hurry to your horse."

. . .

Helena, with a final bow, said, "I won't disobey you, my good lord."

As Helena exited, Bertram turned to Parolles and said, "Go toward home, where I will never return as long as I can wield my sword or hear the drum of war. Let's be off for our escape."

Parolles, eager to support his friend, exclaimed, "Bravely done, courage!"

And with that, they exited together, ready to leave Paris behind.

ACT III

SCENE 1

In the grand palace of the Duke of Florence, the Duke stood with two French lords and a troop of soldiers. The Duke addressed them, "So now you've heard every detail of the reasons for this war, a conflict that has already spilled much blood and still craves more."

The First Lord, loyal to the Duke, said, "The cause seems holy and just on your side, my lord, while it appears dark and terrifying on the enemy's part."

The Duke, puzzled, added, "That's why we're surprised that our cousin, the King of France, would refuse to support us in such a just cause, even when we asked for his help."

. . .

The Second Lord, thoughtful but cautious, replied, "My lord, I cannot speak for the reasons of our state. I'm just an ordinary man, not privy to the decisions made by those in high council. So, I won't say what I think, as I've often been wrong when guessing about such matters."

The Duke nodded, understanding, "Then we must accept it as it is."

The First Lord, more optimistic, said, "But I'm certain that the younger men, who have grown too comfortable, will soon come here seeking the challenge of war as a remedy."

The Duke, welcoming, declared, "They shall be warmly received, and all the honors we can bestow will be theirs. You all know your duties well; when greater opportunities arise, they will fall to your advantage. Tomorrow, we go to the battlefield."

With that, the Duke and his company prepared for the

coming battle. The soldiers and lords left the hall, ready for what lay ahead.

SCENE 2

In the Count's palace at Rousillon, the Countess spoke with the Clown. She expressed her feelings, saying, "Everything has happened just as I wished, except he hasn't come back with her."

The Clown, always quick with a comment, replied, "I swear, I believe our young lord is a very melancholy man."

Curious, the Countess asked, "What makes you think so?"

The Clown explained, "Well, he'll look at his boot and sing; fix his collar and sing; ask questions and sing; even pick his teeth and sing. I once knew a man with the same habit who sold a fine estate for a mere song."

The Countess, still concerned, said, "Let me see what he writes and when he plans to return." She opened a letter from Bertram.

The Clown, thinking of other matters, mused, "I've lost my taste for Isbel ever since I went to court. The Isbels of the country are nothing like those of the court. I'm starting to love like an old man loves money—with little appetite."

The Countess, focused on the letter, read aloud, "I have sent you a daughter-in-law: she has healed the King but ruined me. I have married her, but will never truly be her husband, and I swear to make that 'never' eternal. You'll hear soon that I've run away. Know this before the rumors spread. If there's enough room in the world, I'll keep a long distance. My duty to you, Your unfortunate son, Bertram."

Shocked, the Countess sighed, "This is not well, rash and reckless boy. To flee from the favor of such a good King, to bring his anger upon yourself by scorning a maiden too virtuous even for the contempt of an empire!"

The Clown re-entered, bringing more news. "Oh, madam, there's heavy news inside between two soldiers and my young lady!"

Alarmed, the Countess asked, "What is the matter?"

The Clown, trying to soften the blow, said, "Well, there's some comfort in the news. Your son won't be killed as soon as I thought."

The Countess, concerned, asked, "Why should he be killed?"

The Clown replied, "That's what I say, madam, if he runs away, as I hear he does. The danger is in standing firm—that's how men are lost, even though children might be gained. Here come others who can tell you more. As for me, I've only heard that your son has run away." He exited as Helena entered with two gentlemen.

. . .

The first gentleman greeted her, "Greetings, good madam."

Helena, distraught, announced, "Madam, my lord is gone, forever gone."

The second gentleman tried to comfort her, "Do not say so."

The Countess, trying to remain calm, said, "Think on patience. Please, gentlemen, I've felt so many emotions, both joy and grief, that the first shock of neither can overwhelm me now. Where is my son, I pray you?"

The second gentleman explained, "Madam, he's gone to serve the Duke of Florence. We met him on his way there, for that's where we came from, and after some business at court, we're returning there again."

Helena, holding up the letter, said, "Look at his letter, madam. Here's my passport." She read aloud, "When you can get the ring upon my finger, which will never come off, and show me a child that I am the father of, then call me husband. But in such a 'then,' I write a 'never.' This is a dreadful message."

The Countess asked, "Did you bring this letter, gentlemen?"

The first gentleman replied, "Yes, madam. And we're sorry for the pain its contents cause."

The Countess, turning to Helena, said, "Please, my lady, try to be more cheerful. If you take all the grief upon yourself, you rob me of my share. He was my son, but I wash his name from my blood, and now you are my only child. He's headed toward Florence?"

The second gentleman confirmed, "Yes, madam."

The Countess asked, "And to be a soldier?"

The second gentleman replied, "That is his noble intent, and the Duke will surely honor him as much as is fitting."

. . .

The Countess, still trying to process everything, asked, "Are you returning there?"

The first gentleman answered, "Yes, madam, as quickly as possible."

Helena, reading further, said, "'Till I have no wife, I have nothing in France.' It's bitter."

The Countess, hearing this, asked, "Did you find that there?"

Helena replied, "Yes, madam."

The first gentleman, trying to offer some hope, suggested, "It might just be the boldness of his writing. His heart may not fully agree."

The Countess, deeply saddened, said, "Nothing in France until he has no wife! There's nothing here that's too good for him except her, and she deserves a lord who would be honored to serve her, unlike this rude boy. Who was with him?"

The first gentleman answered, "Only a servant and a gentleman I've known for some time."

The Countess guessed, "Parolles, was it not?"

The first gentleman confirmed, "Yes, my lady, it was he."

The Countess, with disdain, said, "A very corrupt fellow, full of wickedness. My son corrupts his good nature by following him."

The first gentleman agreed, "Indeed, good lady, that man has far too much influence, which he should not have."

The Countess, dismissing them, said, "Thank you, gentlemen. When you see my son, please tell him that his sword can never win back the honor he's lost. I'll write more for you to take along."

. . .

The second gentleman replied, "We are at your service, madam, in this and all your worthy affairs."

The Countess, showing gratitude, said, "Not as much as we exchange our courtesies. Will you come closer?"

The Countess and the gentlemen exited, leaving Helena alone with her thoughts.

Helena, heartbroken, repeated, "'Till I have no wife, I have nothing in France.' Nothing in France until he has no wife! You shall have none, Rousillon, none in France, and then you'll have everything back. Poor lord! Is it I who chase you from your country and expose you to the dangers of war? Is it I who drive you from the playful court, where you were admired, to face the peril of battle? Oh, you deadly messengers of war, those bullets that speed through the air, do not touch my lord. Whoever aims at him, it's as if I placed him there. Whoever charges at him, it's as if I held him to it. And though I do not kill him, I am the cause of his danger. It would be better if I faced a ravenous lion or bore all the world's miseries at once. No, I will go home, Rousillon, where honor may win a scar but often loses all. I will leave. It is my presence here that keeps you away. Shall I stay here to do it? No, no, even if the air of paradise fanned this house and angels served us all, I will go. Let the rumors of my departure bring you comfort. Come, night; end, day! For with the dark, I, poor thief, will steal away."

And with that, Helena left, determined to leave so that Bertram might return home safely.

SCENE 3

Outside the Duke's palace in Florence, the Duke stood with Bertram, Parolles, and a group of soldiers, accompanied by the sound of drums and trumpets. The Duke addressed Bertram with great confidence, saying, "You are now the general of our cavalry, and we place our highest hopes, love, and trust in your promising future."

Bertram, feeling the weight of responsibility, replied, "Sir, this is a heavy burden for my strength, but I will strive to carry it for your worthy sake, even to the greatest risks."

. . .

The Duke, encouraging Bertram, said, "Then go forth, and may fortune favor your helm, like a guiding mistress leading you to success!"

Bertram, determined and ready for battle, declared, "This very day, I dedicate myself to Mars, the god of war. Make me as strong as my thoughts, and I shall become a true follower of the drum, leaving love behind."

With that, they all marched forward, ready to face the challenges ahead.

SCENE 4

In the Count's palace at Rousillon, the Countess was with the Steward, Rinaldo, and she was deeply troubled. "Alas! And you took the letter from her?" she asked. "Did you not realize she would act this way by sending me a letter? Read it to me again."

Rinaldo began to read aloud:

"I am Saint Jaques' pilgrim, thither gone:
    Ambitious love hath so in me offended,
    That barefoot plod I the cold ground upon,
    With sainted vow my faults to have amended.
    Write, write, that from the bloody course of war

My dearest master, your dear son, may hie:
Bless him at home in peace, whilst I from far
His name with zealous fervor sanctify:
His taken labors bid him me forgive;
I, his despiteful Juno, sent him forth
From courtly friends, with camping foes to live,
Where death and danger dogs the heels of worth:
He is too good and fair for death and me:
Whom I myself embrace, to set him free."

The Countess, feeling the pain in Helena's words, sighed, "Ah, what sharp stings are in her mildest words! Rinaldo, you never lacked wisdom so much as when you let her leave like this. Had I spoken with her, I could have changed her mind, but now she's already gone."

Rinaldo, full of regret, replied, "Forgive me, madam. If I had given you the letter last night, she might have been overtaken. But even in her letter, she says pursuit would be in vain."

The Countess, sorrowful, lamented, "What angel shall bless this unworthy husband? He cannot prosper unless her prayers, which heaven delights to hear and loves to grant, save him from the wrath of justice. Write, Rinaldo, write to this undeserving husband of hers. Let every word be filled with the weight of her worth, which he takes too lightly. My greatest grief, though he hardly feels it, should be laid out sharply. Send the quickest messenger. When he hears that she is gone, perhaps he will return. And I hope that when she hears of this, love will guide her back here. Which of them is dearest to me? I cannot tell. Prepare the messenger. My heart is heavy, and my age is weak. Grief would bring tears, and sorrow bids me speak."

With that, they both exited, leaving the Countess burdened with worry and sadness.

SCENE 5

Outside the walls of Florence, the old Widow of Florence, along with Diana, Violenta, Mariana, and other citizens, gathered to watch the arrival of soldiers. The Widow urged, "Come quickly; if they approach the city, we might miss seeing them."

Diana, eager to hear more, added, "They say the French count has performed very honorable service."

The Widow confirmed, "It's reported that he has captured their greatest commander and even killed the Duke's brother with his own hand."

. . .

Suddenly, the sound of a tucket (a trumpet signal) was heard. The Widow sighed, "We have wasted our time; they've gone the other way. Listen! You can tell by the sound of their trumpets."

Mariana suggested, "Let's return and be content with just hearing the reports. But, Diana, be careful of this French earl. A maid's honor is her name, and nothing is as precious as honesty."

The Widow added, "I've already told our neighbor how that gentleman, his companion, has been trying to win your favor."

Mariana, with disdain, said, "I know that rascal—Parolles. He's a disgraceful officer, helping the young earl in these schemes. Beware of them, Diana. Their promises, oaths, and gifts are traps, not what they seem. Many a maid has been deceived by them, but despite the terrible examples, others still fall for the same tricks. I hope you'll stay true to yourself and avoid their snares."

Diana reassured her, "You needn't worry about me."

. . .

The Widow agreed, "I hope so."

Just then, Helena, disguised as a pilgrim, approached. The Widow recognized her and said, "Look, here comes a pilgrim. I know she'll stay at my house; they often send each other there. Let me speak with her." She called out, "God save you, pilgrim! Where are you headed?"

Helena replied, "To Saint Jaques le Grand. Can you tell me where the pilgrims lodge?"

The Widow answered, "At Saint Francis, just by the gate."

Helena asked, "Is this the way?"

The Widow confirmed, "Yes, indeed."

The distant sound of a march reached them, and the Widow continued, "Listen! They're coming this way. If you wait a bit, holy pilgrim, I'll guide you to a place where you can lodge. I think I know your hostess as well as myself."

Helena asked, "Is it yourself?"

The Widow smiled, "If that pleases you, pilgrim."

Helena thanked her, "I thank you and will wait as you wish."

The Widow, curious, asked, "You came from France, I think?"

Helena replied, "I did."

The Widow mentioned, "Here you'll see a countryman of yours who has done worthy service."

Helena inquired, "His name, please?"

Diana answered, "The Count Rousillon. Do you know him?"

. . .

Helena, hiding her true identity, said, "I've heard of him, and only good things, but I don't know his face."

Diana explained, "He's highly regarded here. They say he fled France because the King married him against his will. Do you think that's true?"

Helena, knowing the truth, confirmed, "Yes, it is true. I know his wife."

Diana added, "There's a man serving the Count who speaks poorly of her."

Helena asked, "What's his name?"

Diana replied, "Monsieur Parolles."

Helena remarked, "I'm not surprised. In his praise of the Count or anything else, he wouldn't think her worthy of mention. Her only virtue is her honesty, and I've never heard anyone question that."

Diana sighed, "Poor lady! It must be hard to be the wife of a husband who dislikes her."

The Widow sympathized, "Wherever she is, I'm sure her heart is heavy. This young maid could cause her trouble if she wanted."

Helena, concerned, asked, "What do you mean? Could the Count be pursuing her with improper intentions?"

The Widow confirmed, "He is indeed, and he uses every means he can to corrupt her honor. But she's strong and guards herself well."

Mariana added, "Heaven forbid it should be otherwise!"

The Widow then noticed the soldiers approaching, "Here they come."

. . .

As the drums and colors of the troops became visible, Bertram, Parolles, and the army marched past. The Widow pointed them out, "That's Antonio, the Duke's eldest son; and that's Escalus."

Helena, scanning the soldiers, asked, "Which one is the Frenchman?"

Diana pointed, "That one with the plume. He's a very gallant fellow. I wish he loved his wife. If he were more honest, he'd be even more handsome. Isn't he a fine gentleman?"

Helena, hiding her feelings, said, "I like him well."

Diana, disappointed, said, "It's a pity he's not honest. See that rogue leading him to these places? If I were his wife, I'd poison that vile rascal."

Helena asked, "Which one?"

. . .

Diana pointed again, "That one with the scarves. Why is he so gloomy?"

Helena speculated, "Maybe he's hurt from the battle."

Parolles, passing by, muttered to himself, "We lost our drum! Well."

Mariana noticed his distress, "He's clearly upset about something. Look, he's seen us."

The Widow, unimpressed, muttered, "Let him be."

Mariana added sarcastically, "And your courtesy is as thin as the excuse for that ring you carry."

As the soldiers moved on, the Widow turned to Helena, "The troop has passed. Come, pilgrim, I'll take you to where you'll stay. There are already four or five penitents bound for Saint

Jaques at my house."

Helena thanked her humbly, "I am deeply grateful. Please, may this matron and this gentle maid join us for dinner tonight? I'll cover the cost and offer some advice to this young maiden that might be of value."

The Widow and Diana both agreed, "We'll gladly accept your offer."

And with that, they all left together, heading toward the Widow's home.

SCENE 6

In the camp before Florence, Bertram and two French lords were deep in discussion. The Second Lord encouraged, "Come now, my lord, put him to the test; let him do as he says."

The First Lord added, "If you don't find him to be a coward, then I'm not worthy of your respect."

The Second Lord insisted, "I swear, my lord, he's just a puff of air."

. . .

Bertram, slightly skeptical, asked, "Do you think I'm so wrong about him?"

The Second Lord assured him, "Believe me, my lord, from my own experience, and without any ill will, but only to speak truthfully as his relative, he's a notorious coward, a constant liar, always breaking promises, and lacking any good quality worth your attention."

The First Lord advised, "You should know him well, lest you trust him too much in a critical situation where he might fail you."

Bertram, curious, asked, "But how can I test him in a specific situation?"

The First Lord suggested, "Why not let him retrieve the drum that he so confidently says he'll get back?"

The Second Lord then proposed, "I'll gather a troop of Florentines and surprise him, using men he won't recognize. We'll blindfold and bind him so he believes he's been captured by the enemy. We'll bring him back to our camp, and if, under the threat of death, he doesn't betray you and reveal all the intelligence he knows, swearing on his soul, then never trust my judgment again."

The First Lord, eager for the ruse, said, "For the sake of a good laugh, let him fetch his drum. He claims to have a strategy for it. When you see the outcome and what he's truly made of, if you don't give him the cold shoulder, I'll be surprised. Here he comes now."

Parolles entered, and the Second Lord, whispering to Bertram, said, "For the love of laughter, don't interfere with his plan. Let him try to recover the drum."

Bertram greeted Parolles, "How now, monsieur! It seems this drum is weighing heavily on your mind."

The First Lord dismissed the importance, "Oh, let it go; it's just a drum."

. . .

Parolles, indignant, replied, "'Just a drum'? Is it only 'just a drum'? Losing that drum was a disaster! We ended up attacking our own men!"

The First Lord, unfazed, said, "It wasn't the fault of the command; it was a mishap of war, something even Caesar couldn't have prevented."

Bertram, trying to ease the situation, said, "We can't be too harsh on ourselves for losing that drum; it's not something we can recover."

Parolles, stubborn, insisted, "But it could have been recovered."

Bertram agreed, "Perhaps, but it isn't now."

Parolles, determined, declared, "It can still be recovered. If merit was recognized properly, I'd have that drum or die trying."

. . .

Bertram, testing him, said, "Well, if you have the courage, then go for it, monsieur. If you think your strategy can retrieve that drum, be bold and carry out the mission. I'll support the attempt as a worthy endeavor, and if you succeed, the Duke will surely praise and reward you."

Parolles, full of bravado, promised, "By the hand of a soldier, I'll do it."

Bertram reminded him, "But you must act quickly."

Parolles replied, "I'll start tonight. I'll write out my plan, gather my courage, prepare myself, and by midnight, you'll hear from me."

Bertram, encouraging him, said, "Shall I inform the Duke that you're on your way?"

Parolles, cautious, answered, "I don't know what the outcome will be, my lord, but I vow to make the attempt."

. . .

Bertram, hiding his doubts, said, "I know you're brave, and I'll vouch for your soldierly abilities. Farewell."

Parolles, with a hint of arrogance, responded, "I'm not one for many words."

As Parolles exited, the Second Lord remarked, "No more than a fish loves water. Isn't it strange, my lord, that he's so confident in taking on a task he knows he can't accomplish, yet he'd rather be damned than admit it?"

The First Lord explained, "You don't know him like we do, my lord. He has a way of sneaking into people's favor and avoiding discovery for a while, but once you see through him, you'll never trust him again."

Bertram asked, "Do you think he'll do nothing at all, despite how seriously he talks about it?"

The Second Lord replied, "Nothing in the world, except come back with a made-up story and a few convincing lies. But we've almost trapped him; you'll see his downfall tonight. He's not worthy of your respect."

The First Lord added, "We'll have some fun with this fox before we unmask him. He was first exposed by old Lord Lafeu. Once his disguise is stripped away, you'll see what a small fish he really is, and you'll see it tonight."

The Second Lord then said, "I must go prepare; he'll be caught."

Bertram agreed, "Your brother shall go with me."

The Second Lord replied, "As you wish, my lord," and exited.

Bertram, turning to the First Lord, said, "Now, I'll take you to see the lady I spoke of."

The First Lord, curious, asked, "But you said she's honest?"

· · ·

Bertram sighed, "That's the only problem. I spoke with her just once, and she was very cold to me. But I sent her tokens and letters through that fool we've just talked about, and she returned them all. That's all I've done. She's a fair creature. Will you go see her?"

The First Lord replied, "With all my heart, my lord."

And with that, they exited together.

SCENE 7

In the Widow's house in Florence, Helena and the Widow were engaged in a serious conversation. Helena, sensing the Widow's hesitation, said, "If you doubt that I am who I say I am, I don't know how else I can convince you without losing the plan I've been working on."

The Widow, concerned about her reputation, replied, "Though my circumstances have declined, I come from a good family. I've never been involved in such matters before and wouldn't want to risk my reputation now."

Helena reassured her, "Nor would I ask you to. First, trust me—Count Bertram is my husband. What I've shared with you in confidence is true, word for word. With your help, we won't go wrong in carrying out this plan."

The Widow, starting to believe her, said, "I should trust you, for you've shown me proof that you are indeed fortunate."

Helena handed the Widow a purse of gold, saying, "Take this gold, and let me buy your friendly help. I will repay you many times over. The Count is pursuing your daughter, determined to win her. Let her agree to his advances, as we'll instruct her on the best way to do it. In his passion, he won't deny her anything she asks, including a ring he wears, which has been passed down in his family for four or five generations. He values it highly, yet in his desire, he might give it up, even if he regrets it later."

The Widow, now understanding Helena's plan, said, "I see the purpose behind your request."

Helena continued, "You see it's lawful, then. Your daughter should agree to his advances but ask for the ring first. She'll arrange a meeting with him but will secretly let me take her place, while she remains chaste and absent. Once this is done, I'll give her an additional three thousand crowns on top of what I've already given you."

The Widow, agreeing to the plan, said, "I agree. Teach my daughter how to proceed so that time and place work together with this lawful deception. Every night he comes with musicians and songs, serenading her. It does no good to chase him away, for he persists as if his life depends on it."

Helena, ready to move forward, said, "Then let's carry out our plan tonight. If it succeeds, we'll have turned his wicked intent into a lawful act. Both of us remain innocent, though the deed may seem otherwise. But enough talk—let's begin."

With that, they left to set their plan in motion.

ACT IV

SCENE 1

Outside the Florentine camp, the Second French Lord hid in ambush with five or six soldiers. He explained the plan, "He can only come this way by the hedge-corner. When we attack, speak in whatever frightening language you can muster. Even if you don't understand it yourself, it doesn't matter—we must pretend we don't understand him unless we produce someone as an interpreter."

One of the soldiers eagerly volunteered, "Good captain, let me be the interpreter."

. . .

The Second Lord questioned, "Aren't you familiar with him? Doesn't he know your voice?"

The soldier reassured him, "No, sir, I assure you he does not."

The Second Lord asked, "And what nonsense will you speak back to us?"

The soldier confidently replied, "The same kind of nonsense you speak to me."

The Second Lord continued, "He must think we're a band of foreign soldiers. He has a bit of knowledge of various languages, so each of us must speak something different. As long as we seem to know what we're saying, our purpose will be clear. Just enough gibberish to make it believable. And you, interpreter, must act very clever. But quiet now—here he comes, probably thinking he can kill some time in sleep before returning with a pack of lies."

Parolles entered, speaking to himself, "It's ten o'clock. In three hours, it'll be time to go home. What shall I say I've done? It has to be a very convincing lie to pull this off. They're starting to suspect me, and I've been facing too many embarrassments lately. My tongue has been too reckless, but my heart is too fearful of Mars and his warriors to back it up."

The Second Lord, hidden, remarked, "That's the first honest thing your tongue has ever said."

Parolles continued, unaware of the ambush, "Why on earth did I decide to recover this drum? I knew it was impossible and had no intention of actually doing it! I'll have to injure myself and claim I got the wounds during the mission. But slight wounds won't be enough; they'll ask, 'Did you escape with just that?' And I can't give myself serious wounds. What to do? Tongue, I'll have to replace you with something less foolish, like the bridle of Bajazet's mule, if you keep getting me into these predicaments."

The Second Lord, still listening, whispered, "Is it possible he knows what a fraud he is, yet remains one?"

. . .

Parolles, pacing, continued, "If only tearing my clothes or breaking my sword would be enough."

The Second Lord whispered again, "We can't let you off so easily."

Parolles went on, "Or if shaving my beard could count as a strategy."

The Second Lord commented, "That won't work."

Parolles, desperate, said, "Or if soaking my clothes and claiming I was stripped would suffice."

The Second Lord whispered, "That won't do, either."

Parolles, getting more desperate, said, "Even if I swore I jumped out of the citadel window—"

The Second Lord asked, "How deep?"

. . .

Parolles guessed, "Thirty fathoms."

The Second Lord, amused, said, "Three great oaths wouldn't make that believable."

Parolles, resigned, said, "I wish I had an enemy's drum. I'd swear I recovered it."

The Second Lord, preparing the ambush, signaled, "You'll hear one soon."

Suddenly, an alarm sounded within the camp, and the Second Lord shouted in a made-up language, "Throca movousus, cargo, cargo, cargo."

The soldiers echoed, "Cargo, cargo, cargo, villiando par corbo, cargo."

. . .

Panicking, Parolles cried out, "Ransom, ransom! Don't blindfold me!"

The soldiers seized him and covered his eyes. One soldier continued the gibberish, "Boskos thromuldo boskos."

Parolles, terrified, said, "I know you're from the Muskos regiment! I'll die here if no one understands me. If there's a German, Dane, Dutch, Italian, or Frenchman among you, speak to me! I'll reveal secrets that will ruin the Florentines."

The soldier, pretending to understand, responded, "Boskos vauvado: I understand you. Sir, prepare yourself; seventeen daggers are pointed at your chest."

Parolles, trembling, exclaimed, "O!"

The soldier continued, "Pray, pray, pray! Manka revania dulche."

. . .

The Second Lord added more gibberish, "Oscorbidulchos volivorco."

The soldier, pretending to show mercy, said, "The general is willing to spare you for now. Blindfolded as you are, we'll lead you on to gather information. Maybe you can save your life."

Parolles, desperate, begged, "Oh, let me live! I'll tell you all the secrets of our camp, their forces, their plans. I'll tell you things that will amaze you."

The soldier asked, "But will you do it faithfully?"

Parolles swore, "If I don't, may I be damned."

The soldier responded, "Acordo linta. Come on; you have some time."

They led Parolles away under guard. After a short alarm within the camp, the Second Lord ordered, "Go, tell Count

Rousillon and my brother that we've caught the fool, and we'll keep him blindfolded until we hear from them."

Another soldier replied, "Captain, I will."

The Second Lord, knowing Parolles' true nature, said, "He'll betray us all to our own advantage. Make sure to report that."

The soldier answered, "I will, sir."

The Second Lord concluded, "Until then, I'll keep him hidden and safely locked up."

With that, they all exited, leaving Parolles trapped in his own lies.

SCENE 2

At the Widow's house in Florence, Bertram was speaking with Diana. "They told me your name was Fontibell," he began.

Diana corrected him, "No, my good lord, Diana."

Bertram, admiring her, said, "A name fit for a goddess, and you're worthy of the title! But tell me, fair soul, does love not touch your heart? If the fiery passion of youth doesn't spark your mind, then you're not a living maiden but a cold monument. When you're dead, you should look just as you do now, for you are cold and stern. Now, you should be as your mother was when you were conceived."

. . .

Diana replied with dignity, "She was honest then."

Bertram pressed on, "And so should you be."

Diana held her ground, "No, my lord. My mother did her duty, just as you owe a duty to your wife."

Bertram, brushing off her words, said, "No more of that. Please, don't resist my vows. I was forced into marriage with her, but I love you by the sweet constraint of love itself and will forever serve you."

Diana responded sharply, "You serve us only until you've taken what you want, and then you leave us with nothing but the thorns to prick ourselves, mocking our emptiness."

Bertram protested, "But I've sworn!"

. . .

Diana wisely said, "It's not the many oaths that make something true, but the single honest vow. We don't swear by what is unholy; we swear by the highest power. So tell me, if I swore by God's great attributes that I loved you, would you believe me if I didn't? To swear by Him and then act against Him is senseless. Your oaths are just empty words, meaningless unless sealed with true intention."

Bertram, trying to sway her, said, "Change your mind, don't be so cruel. Love is holy, and I have never been deceitful like you accuse men of being. Don't resist any longer; give in to my desires, and I'll be healed. Say you are mine, and my love will stay true."

Diana, seeing through his intentions, asked, "I see that men often weave lies to trap us. Give me that ring."

Bertram hesitated, "I'll lend it to you, my dear, but I can't give it away."

Diana questioned, "Won't you, my lord?"

. . .

Bertram explained, "It's an honor belonging to my family, passed down through many generations. It would be the greatest disgrace for me to lose it."

Diana countered, "My honor is like that ring. My chastity is the jewel of my family, passed down through many generations. It would be the greatest disgrace for me to lose it. So your own wisdom now stands in defense of my honor, against your attempt to take it."

Bertram, feeling the weight of her words, relented, "Here, take my ring. My family, my honor, even my life, are yours, and I'll do as you command."

Diana, setting her plan in motion, said, "When midnight comes, knock at my chamber window. I'll make sure my mother doesn't hear. But I must insist on one condition: after you've claimed my bed, stay there only for an hour, and don't speak to me. My reasons are strong, and you'll understand them when I return this ring to you. During the night, I'll place another ring on your finger that will symbolize what we've done. Farewell until then; don't fail to come. You have won a wife in me, though that's where my hope ends."

• • •

Bertram, overjoyed, said, "I've won a heaven on earth by wooing you." He then exited, leaving Diana alone.

Once he was gone, Diana spoke to herself, "For that, may you live long to thank both heaven and me! My mother told me exactly how he would woo, as if she knew his heart. She says all men make the same oaths. He swore to marry me when his wife is dead; so I'll lie with him only when I'm buried. Since Frenchmen are so deceitful, I'll live and die a maid. But in this disguise, I think it's no sin to deceive the man who would unjustly win me."

With her plan in place, Diana also exited, ready to outsmart Bertram.

SCENE 3

In the Florentine camp, the two French Lords were discussing recent events with a few soldiers. The First Lord asked, "You haven't given him his mother's letter yet?"

The Second Lord replied, "I delivered it an hour ago. Something in that letter really shook him; he changed completely after reading it."

The First Lord sighed, "He's been rightly blamed for abandoning such a good wife and sweet lady."

. . .

The Second Lord added, "Especially since he's now facing the king's everlasting displeasure. The king had been so generous to him, hoping to bring him happiness. I'll tell you something, but keep it to yourself."

The First Lord assured him, "Once you've spoken it, it's dead, and I'll keep it secret."

The Second Lord revealed, "He has seduced a young woman here in Florence, a girl known for her chastity. Tonight, he plans to destroy her honor. He's given her the family ring he treasures so much and thinks this will complete his unholy conquest."

The First Lord, dismayed, remarked, "God save us from our own rebellion! We are our own worst enemies."

The Second Lord agreed, "Indeed, we often betray ourselves. Just as treason eventually reveals itself, his actions betray his own nobility."

. . .

The First Lord reflected, "Is it not sinful for us to trumpet our wrongful intentions? So, we won't see him tonight?"

The Second Lord responded, "Not until after midnight; he has a strict schedule."

The First Lord observed, "That time is approaching quickly. I wish he could see the consequences of his actions, to measure the depth of his misjudgments and how thoroughly he has been deceived by that counterfeit."

The Second Lord replied, "We'll wait until he arrives; his presence is necessary for what's to come."

The First Lord shifted the topic, asking, "What news do you hear of the war?"

The Second Lord answered, "I've heard there's talk of peace."

The First Lord corrected, "No, peace has already been concluded."

. . .

The Second Lord wondered, "What will Count Rousillon do now? Will he travel elsewhere, or return to France?"

The First Lord, suspecting something, said, "I see by your question that you're not privy to his plans."

The Second Lord responded, "Heaven forbid, for then I'd be too involved in his actions."

The First Lord explained, "His wife fled from his house about two months ago, claiming she was on a pilgrimage to Saint Jaques le Grand. She completed that holy journey with the utmost devotion, but in the end, grief overtook her, and she died. Now, she sings in heaven."

The Second Lord, surprised, asked, "How is this confirmed?"

The First Lord answered, "Most of it is confirmed by her own letters, which tell the story up to her death. The actual fact of her death was confirmed by the local priest."

. . .

The Second Lord asked, "Does the Count know all of this?"

The First Lord replied, "Yes, and he has all the details, point by point, confirming the truth."

The Second Lord, saddened, said, "I'm sorry to think that he'll be glad of this news."

The First Lord mused, "How strange it is that sometimes we find comfort in our losses!"

The Second Lord added, "And how strange that other times we drown our gains in tears! The great honor he's won here will be met with equal shame at home."

The First Lord reflected, "The fabric of our lives is a mix of good and bad. Our virtues would grow proud without our faults to humble them, and our crimes would lead us to despair without our virtues to redeem them."

. . .

A messenger entered, and the First Lord asked, "How now! Where's your master?"

The messenger replied, "He met the Duke in the street, sir, and took a solemn leave of him. His lordship will leave for France tomorrow morning. The Duke has offered him letters of commendation to the king."

The Second Lord commented, "Those letters will be very necessary, even if they're full of praise."

The First Lord added, "They can't be too sweet to soften the king's harshness. Here comes his lordship now."

Bertram entered, and the First Lord greeted him, "How now, my lord! Is it not after midnight?"

Bertram replied, "Tonight, I've taken care of sixteen matters, each one a month's work, all done with successful results. I've bid farewell to the Duke, said goodbye to his closest allies, mourned for my wife, written to my mother that I'm returning, arranged my journey home, and dealt with many other tasks. The last one was the greatest, but it's not finished yet."

The Second Lord suggested, "If it's difficult and you're leaving in the morning, your lordship must act quickly."

Bertram explained, "I mean, the business isn't over, and I fear hearing more about it later. But shall we have this dialogue between the fool and the soldier? Bring forth the counterfeit; he's deceived me, like a double-meaning prophet."

The Second Lord replied, "Bring him forth. He's been in the stocks all night, poor fool."

Bertram, unconcerned, said, "No matter, his feet deserved it for pretending to be a soldier for so long. How is he behaving?"

. . .

The Second Lord replied, "I've told your lordship already, the stocks are holding him up. But to answer as you'd expect: he weeps like a milkmaid who's lost her milk. He's confessed everything to Morgan, whom he thinks is a friar, from his earliest memory to his current disaster. What do you think he's confessed?"

Bertram, worried, asked, "Nothing about me, has he?"

The Second Lord answered, "His confession has been taken down, and it will be read to him. If your lordship is mentioned, as I believe you are, you must be patient and listen."

Parolles was brought in, blindfolded and guarded, by the First Soldier. Bertram, frustrated, muttered, "A plague upon him! He's blindfolded; he can't say anything about me. Hush, hush!"

The First Lord, amused, exclaimed, "Hoodman comes! Portotartarosa!"

. . .

The First Soldier, playing along, asked, "He's asking for tortures. What will you say without them?"

Parolles, terrified, said, "I'll confess what I know without being tortured. If you pinch me like a pasty, I can't say any more."

The First Soldier spoke in gibberish, "Bosko chimurcho."

The First Lord continued the farce, "Boblibindo chicurmurco."

The First Soldier addressed Parolles, "You are a merciful general. Our general bids you answer what I ask from this note."

Parolles, eager to comply, promised, "And truly, as I hope to live."

The First Soldier read from the note, "First, demand of him how many horse the Duke has. What say you to that?"

. . .

Parolles quickly replied, "Five or six thousand, but they're very weak and unserviceable. The troops are scattered, and the commanders are poor rogues, on my reputation and credit, and as I hope to live."

The First Soldier asked, "Shall I write that down?"

Parolles eagerly agreed, "Do so. I'll swear to it, whichever way you like."

Bertram, disgusted, commented, "All's the same to him. What a hopeless scoundrel he is!"

The First Lord observed, "You're mistaken, my lord. This is Monsieur Parolles, the gallant soldier who claimed to have the entire theory of war tied up in his scarf, and all the practice in the tip of his dagger."

The Second Lord added, "I'll never trust a man again just because he keeps his sword clean, nor believe he's competent just because he dresses neatly."

The First Soldier confirmed, "That's written down."

Parolles, anxious to provide more information, said, "Five or six thousand horse, I said. I'll say it's true—or thereabouts. Write it down, for I'll speak the truth."

The First Lord admitted, "He's close to the truth on this."

Bertram, unimpressed, said, "But I give him no credit for the way he delivers it."

Parolles added, "Poor rogues, please write that down."

The First Soldier did so, and Parolles thanked him, "I humbly thank you, sir. Truth is truth, and the rogues are indeed poor."

. . .

The First Soldier continued reading from the note, "Demand of him what strength they have on foot. What say you to that?"

Parolles, pretending to think, replied, "By my word, sir, if I were to live another hour, I'll tell the truth. Let me see: Spurio, a hundred and fifty; Sebastian, so many; Corambus, so many; Jaques, so many; Guiltian, Cosmo, Lodowick, and Gratii, two hundred and fifty each; my own company, Chitopher, Vaumond, Bentii, two hundred and fifty each. So, the total muster, rotten and sound, amounts to no more than fifteen thousand. Half of them wouldn't even dare shake snow off their coats, lest they shake themselves to pieces."

Bertram, growing tired of the charade, asked, "What shall we do with him?"

The First Lord suggested, "Nothing, but give him thanks. Ask him about my standing and credit with the Duke."

The First Soldier agreed, "Well, that's written down."

. . .

He continued reading

, "You shall ask him whether one Captain Dumain is in the camp, a Frenchman; what his reputation is with the Duke; what his valor, honesty, and expertise in war are; or whether he thinks it's possible to bribe him to defect with enough gold. What say you to this? What do you know of it?"

Parolles, nervous, pleaded, "Please, let me answer these questions one by one."

The First Soldier asked, "Do you know this Captain Dumain?"

Parolles, inventing more lies, replied, "I know him. He was a tailor's apprentice in Paris, whipped for getting the sheriff's fool with child—a mute girl who couldn't say no."

Bertram, furious, intervened, "Hold your tongue! Even though I know his brains are forfeit to the next tile that falls."

. . .

The First Soldier continued, "Well, is this Captain Dumain in the Duke of Florence's camp?"

Parolles confirmed, "Yes, upon my knowledge, and he's filthy."

The First Lord warned, "Don't look at me like that; we'll hear more about your lordship soon."

The First Soldier asked, "What is his reputation with the Duke?"

Parolles lied, "The Duke knows him only as a poor officer of mine and wrote to me the other day to have him dismissed. I think I have the letter in my pocket."

The First Soldier searched him, saying, "Let's see."

Parolles panicked, "In all seriousness, I'm not sure. It's either here or filed with the Duke's other letters in my tent."

. . .

The First Soldier found a paper and asked, "Here it is; shall I read it?"

Parolles, anxious, replied, "I don't know if that's it or not."

Bertram whispered to the First Lord, "Our interpreter is doing well."

The First Lord agreed, "Excellently."

The First Soldier read aloud, "Dian, the Count is a fool, and full of gold—"

Parolles interrupted, "That's not the Duke's letter, sir. That's a note to a young woman in Florence, one Diana, warning her to avoid the advances of Count Rousillon, a foolish, idle boy, but very lustful. Please, sir, put it away."

The First Soldier insisted, "No, I'll read it first."

. . .

Parolles protested, "I meant it honestly, sir, in the girl's best interest. I knew the young Count was dangerous and lascivious, a predator to virginity."

Bertram, enraged, muttered, "Damnable traitor!"

The First Soldier continued reading, "When he swears oaths, bid him drop gold, and take it; after he scores, he never pays the score: half won is match well made; match, and well make it; he ne'er pays after-debts, take it before; and say a soldier, Dian, told thee this, men are to mell with, boys are not to kiss: for count of this, the Count's a fool, I know it, who pays before, but not when he does owe it. Thine, as he vowed to thee in thine ear, Parolles."

Bertram, seething with anger, declared, "He shall be whipped through the army with this rhyme on his forehead."

The Second Lord remarked sarcastically, "This is your devoted friend, sir, the expert linguist and mighty soldier."

. . .

Bertram, disgusted, said, "I could endure anything before, even a cat, but now he's worse than a cat to me."

The First Soldier noted, "I see by the general's expression that we'll have to hang you."

Parolles, terrified, pleaded, "My life, sir, in any case! Not that I'm afraid to die, but because I have many sins to repent. Let me live, sir, even if it's in a dungeon or the stocks, anywhere, as long as I live."

The First Soldier decided, "We'll see what can be done if you confess freely. Now, once more about this Captain Dumain: you've answered about his reputation and valor, but what about his honesty?"

Parolles slandered, "He'll steal an egg from a cloister. He's as bad as Nessus for rapes and ravishments. He breaks oaths stronger than Hercules. He lies so skillfully you'd think truth was a fool. Drunkenness is his best quality, for he'll be as drunk as a pig. In his sleep, he only harms his bedclothes. But they know his ways and lay him on straw. I have little more to say about his honesty: he has none of the qualities an honest man should have and all the qualities he shouldn't."

The First Lord, amused, said, "I'm beginning to like him for this."

Bertram, still angry, said, "For this description of honesty? A curse on him; he's still a cat to me."

The First Soldier asked, "What about his expertise in war?"

Parolles dismissed him, "He's led the drum before the English actors, but I won't lie. I know little of his soldiering, except he once had the honor of being an officer at a place called Mile-End, to teach the doubling of files. I'd give him what honor I can, but I'm not certain."

The First Lord observed, "He's outdone villainy so much that it's almost redeeming."

Bertram cursed again, "A pox on him; he's still a cat."

. . .

The First Soldier, concluding, asked, "With his qualities being so poor, I need not ask if gold would tempt him to betray his side."

Parolles confirmed, "For a quart d'ecu, he'd sell his soul and cut off all ties to salvation."

The First Soldier asked, "And what of his brother, the other Captain Dumain?"

The Second Lord whispered, "Why does he ask him about me?"

The First Soldier repeated, "What about him?"

Parolles continued his lies, "He's from the same nest, not as bad as the first but still very wicked. He's a greater coward than his brother, who's reputed as one of the best. In a retreat, he outruns any lackey; in battle, he has the cramp."

. . .

The First Soldier asked, "If your life is spared, will you betray the Florentine?"

Parolles agreed, "Yes, and the captain of his horse, Count Rousillon."

The First Soldier whispered to the Second Lord, "I'll confer with the general and know his decision."

Parolles, in despair, muttered to himself, "I'll no more drumming; a plague on all drums! I only pretended to be deserving to fool that lascivious young Count. Who would have suspected an ambush where I was caught?"

The First Soldier returned and declared, "There is no remedy, sir; you must die. The general says you've betrayed the secrets of your army and slandered noble men, so you must die. Come, executioner, off with his head."

Parolles, panicked, pleaded, "O Lord, sir, let me live, or at least let me see my death!"

. . .

The First Lord, deciding it was time, said, "That you shall, and take your leave of all your friends."

They removed the blindfold, and Parolles saw the lords and soldiers around him.

Bertram greeted him mockingly, "Good morning, noble captain."

The Second Lord added, "God bless you, Captain Parolles."

The First Lord joined in, "God save you, noble captain."

The Second Lord teased, "Captain, what message would you send to my Lord Lafeu? I'm heading for France."

The First Lord continued, "Good captain, will you give me a copy of the sonnet you wrote to Diana on behalf of Count Rousillon? If I weren't such a coward, I'd compel it from you. Farewell."

. . .

Bertram and the lords exited, leaving Parolles humiliated.

The First Soldier told him, "You're ruined, captain, all but your scarf; that still has a knot on it."

Parolles, defeated, asked, "Who can't be crushed by a plot?"

The First Soldier replied, "If you could find a country where only women who have been so shamed live, you might start an impudent nation. Farewell, sir; I'm off to France too. We'll talk about you there."

The soldiers exited, leaving Parolles alone.

Parolles, reflecting on his fate, said, "Yet I'm thankful. If my heart were great, it would burst from this. Captain I'll be no more; but I'll eat, drink, and sleep as comfortably as a captain. Simply being myself will keep me alive. Who knows he's a braggart, let him fear this, for it will happen that every braggart will be found a fool. Rust, sword! Cool, blushes! And Parolles, live safely in shame! Being fooled, thrive on foolishness! There's a place and means for every man alive. I'll follow them."

He exited, determined to survive despite his disgrace.

SCENE 4

In the Widow's house in Florence, Helena spoke earnestly to the Widow and Diana, trying to reassure them. "So that you may understand I haven't wronged you, one of the greatest rulers in the Christian world will vouch for me. Before his throne, I must kneel to complete my plans. Once, I did him a service that was almost as dear to him as life itself, and even the hardest heart would feel gratitude and respond with thanks. I've been informed that his grace, the King, is in Marseilles, and we have a safe way to get there. You must know that I am believed to be dead. The army is disbanding, and my husband is heading home. With heaven's help, and with the King's permission, we'll arrive before he expects us."

. . .

The Widow, touched by Helena's sincerity, replied, "Gentle madam, you've never had a servant who was more eager to help you."

Helena, equally grateful, responded, "And you've never had a friend whose thoughts worked more sincerely to repay your kindness. Don't doubt that heaven has brought me to be your daughter's dowry, just as it has destined her to be my guide and helper to a husband. But how strange men are! They can find sweet pleasure in things they hate, and when they deceive themselves, they soil the night with their unworthy desires. Lust plays with what it despises because it can't have what it truly wants. But enough of that for now. Diana, under my guidance, you may have to endure something on my behalf."

Diana, loyal and brave, replied, "Let death and honesty come with your commands; I am yours, ready to endure whatever you ask."

Helena, grateful for Diana's commitment, said, "I pray you, be patient. The time will come when even the harsh briers will bear leaves as well as thorns and will be as sweet as they are sharp. We must go now; our wagon is ready, and it's time for us to leave. All's well that ends well; the end justifies the journey, and whatever the path, the outcome is what truly matters."

With their plans set, they all exited, ready to take the next step in their journey.

SCENE 5

In the Count's palace at Rousillon, the Countess, Lafeu, and the Clown were engaged in conversation. Lafeu, reflecting on recent events, said, "No, no, no, your son was misled by that flashy, worthless fellow, who could have turned all the young, impressionable men of the nation into his gaudy image. If not for that red-tailed rogue I mentioned, your daughter-in-law would still be alive, and your son would be here at home, more honored by the king than by that deceitful rascal."

The Countess, filled with sorrow, responded, "I wish I had never known him. It was the death of the most virtuous woman nature ever created. Even if she had been my own flesh and blood, and I had borne her with the deepest pain, I couldn't have loved her more deeply."

Lafeu, echoing her sentiment, said, "She was a good lady, truly a good lady. We could search through a thousand fields and never find another herb like her."

The Clown, trying to lighten the mood, added, "Indeed, sir, she was the sweet marjoram of the salad, or rather, the herb of grace."

Lafeu, correcting him, said, "They are not herbs, you knave; they are nose-herbs."

The Clown quipped, "I'm no great Nebuchadnezzar, sir; I don't have much skill in grass."

Lafeu, amused, asked, "Do you consider yourself a knave or a fool?"

. . .

The Clown replied, "A fool, sir, when serving a woman, and a knave when serving a man."

Lafeu inquired further, "What's the distinction?"

The Clown answered, "I would trick the man out of his wife and then serve him."

Lafeu chuckled, "So you would indeed be a knave in his service."

The Clown added with a grin, "And I would give his wife my bauble to serve her."

Lafeu, acknowledging the Clown's wit, said, "I'll vouch for you; you're both a knave and a fool."

The Clown responded with a playful bow, "At your service."

Lafeu, amused, replied, "No, no, no."

. . .

The Clown continued, "Well, sir, if I can't serve you, I can serve a prince as great as you."

Lafeu, intrigued, asked, "Who's that? A Frenchman?"

The Clown, with a hint of mischief, answered, "Faith, sir, he has an English name, but his reputation is hotter in France than there."

Lafeu, curious, asked, "What prince is that?"

The Clown, revealing the joke, said, "The black prince, sir; also known as the prince of darkness, or the devil."

Lafeu, laughing, handed the Clown his purse, saying, "Here, take this. I'm not giving it to encourage you to leave your master, the one you just mentioned. Keep serving him."

. . .

The Clown, delighted, said, "I'm a man who always loved a good fire, and my master keeps one burning. But surely, he's the prince of the world; let his nobility stay in his court. I'm for the house with the narrow gate, too small for pomp to enter. Some who humble themselves may pass through, but most will be too cold and tender and choose the wide, flowery path that leads to the broad gate and the great fire."

Lafeu, growing tired of the banter, said, "Go on your way. I'm starting to get weary of you, and I tell you this now so we won't fall out with each other. Go on your way, and make sure my horses are well taken care of, with no tricks."

The Clown, leaving, said, "If I play any tricks on them, sir, they'll be the tricks of jades, which are their natural right by law."

After the Clown exited, Lafeu commented, "A clever knave, but troublesome."

The Countess agreed, "So he is. My late husband found much amusement in him, and by his authority, he stays here, thinking it gives him a license for his impudence. He doesn't walk but runs wherever he pleases."

Lafeu, finding the Clown amusing, said, "I like him well enough; he's not so bad. But I wanted to tell you, since I heard of the good lady's death and that your son was on his way home, I spoke to the king on behalf of my daughter. The king, remembering a proposal he made when they were both younger, has promised to bring it to fruition. It will also help to mend the king's displeasure with your son. What do you think of it?"

The Countess, pleased, responded, "I am very content, my lord, and I hope it comes to pass happily."

Lafeu added, "The king is coming from Marseilles, as fit and strong as when he was thirty. He'll be here tomorrow unless I'm mistaken by my source, who rarely fails in such matters."

The Countess, overjoyed, said, "It gladdens me, for I hope to see him before I die. I've received letters that my son will arrive tonight. I'll ask your lordship to stay with me until they meet."

Lafeu, considering, said, "Madam, I was wondering how I might be safely admitted."

The Countess reassured him, "You need only claim your honorable privilege."

Lafeu, grateful, said, "Lady, I've made bold use of that privilege, but thank God it still holds."

The Clown re-entered with news, "O madam, your son is here with a patch of velvet on his face. Whether there's a scar under it or not, the velvet knows. But it's a goodly patch of velvet. His left cheek is as smooth as two layers of velvet, but his right cheek is worn bare."

Lafeu, seeing the humor, said, "A scar nobly earned, or a noble scar, is a badge of honor. It seems that's what he has."

The Clown, ever the jester, added, "But his face looks like it's been sliced up."

. . .

Lafeu, eager to see Bertram, said, "Let's go see your son. I long to speak with the young noble soldier."

The Clown, with a flourish, concluded, "Faith, there's a dozen of them, all wearing delicate fine hats with the most courteous feathers, nodding at every man."

With that, they all exited to greet Bertram.

ACT V

SCENE 1

In a street in Marseilles, Helena, the Widow, and Diana, accompanied by two attendants, hurriedly discussed their journey. Helena, noticing the weariness of her companions, said, "This relentless travel, day and night, must be wearing you down, but we have no choice. You've been tireless in my service, and I hope you'll see that your efforts grow into a reward that nothing can take away."

Just then, a gentleman appeared. Spotting him, Helena brightened, "In good time! This man might help me reach the king's ear. God save you, sir."

The Gentleman politely responded, "And you."

. . .

Helena, recognizing him, said, "Sir, I've seen you at the court of France."

The Gentleman acknowledged, "I've been there at times."

Helena, hopeful, continued, "I trust your reputation for goodness hasn't faded. Urged by pressing needs that leave little room for formality, I appeal to your virtues, and I will remain ever grateful."

The Gentleman asked, "What do you need?"

Helena explained, "I hope you'll deliver this humble petition to the king and use your influence to help me gain an audience with him."

The Gentleman informed her, "The king isn't here."

Surprised, Helena asked, "Not here, sir?"

. . .

The Gentleman confirmed, "Indeed, no. He left last night, and in more haste than usual."

The Widow, disheartened, exclaimed, "Lord, how we've wasted our efforts!"

Helena, trying to stay positive, said, "All's well that ends well, yet, even though time seems against us and the means aren't perfect. Please, sir, where has he gone?"

The Gentleman replied, "As I understand, to Rousillon. That's where I'm headed."

Helena, seizing the opportunity, said, "I beg you, sir, since you'll see the king before I do, deliver this paper to his gracious hand. I'm sure it will bring you no blame, but rather, earn you thanks for your efforts. I'll follow as quickly as I can."

The Gentleman assured her, "I'll do this for you."

Helena, grateful, said, "And you'll find yourself well thanked, no matter what else happens. We must get back on our horses. Go, go, make ready."

With that, they all quickly made their preparations to continue their journey to Rousillon, determined to reach the king.

SCENE 2

Outside the Count's palace in Rousillon, Parolles approached the Clown, known as Monsieur Lavache. "Good Monsieur Lavache, please give this letter to Lord Lafeu," Parolles requested. "You knew me better before when I was dressed in finer clothes, but now, I'm covered in the mud of misfortune and bear the heavy scent of her displeasure."

The Clown, ever ready with a witty retort, replied, "Well, if fortune's displeasure smells as bad as you say, then she must be quite filthy. I won't be eating anything that fortune has buttered from now on. Step aside, please."

. . .

Parolles tried to explain, "You needn't hold your nose, sir; I was speaking metaphorically."

But the Clown, unimpressed, shot back, "If your metaphor stinks, I'll still hold my nose. Get away from me."

Parolles persisted, "Please, sir, deliver this paper for me."

The Clown, disgusted, said, "Foh! Stand back. A letter from the toilet of fortune to give to a nobleman? Look, here comes the lord himself."

As Lafeu entered, the Clown continued, "Here's a poor creature, muddied and miserable, who claims to be a victim of fortune's displeasure. He's like a carp caught in a dirty pond. I'll leave him to your mercy, sir, though I pity him."

The Clown then exited, leaving Parolles to face Lafeu.

Parolles, attempting to garner sympathy, said, "My lord, I am a man whom fortune has cruelly scratched."

. . .

Lafeu, unmoved, asked, "And what would you have me do? It's too late to trim her nails now. How have you wronged fortune to deserve her scratch? She's usually a kind lady and doesn't let knaves thrive long. Here's a small coin for you; let the justices reconcile you with fortune. I have other matters to attend to."

Parolles pleaded, "I beg your honor to hear just one word."

Lafeu, sensing another plea for charity, said, "You're asking for more than a word. Here, take this, but save your breath."

Parolles introduced himself, hoping to remind Lafeu of their past, "My name, my good lord, is Parolles."

Lafeu, feigning surprise, said, "Ah, you're asking for more than just a word! Give me your hand. How is your drum?"

Parolles, with a touch of desperation, responded, "O my good lord, you were the first to see through me!"

. . .

Lafeu, with mock surprise, said, "Was I indeed? And I was the first to lose you too."

Parolles, trying to gain favor, said, "It's within your power, my lord, to restore my standing, as you were the one who exposed me."

Lafeu, sternly, replied, "Out upon you, knave! Do you expect me to play both God and the devil? One brings you grace, the other casts you out."

At that moment, the sound of trumpets heralded the King's arrival. Lafeu, hearing the trumpets, said, "The King is coming. I know it by the sound of his trumpets. Sirrah, seek me out later; I spoke of you last night. Even though you're a fool and a knave, you shall still eat. Now, follow."

Parolles, with a sigh of relief, replied, "I praise God for you."

. . .

Both Lafeu and Parolles exited, following the sound of the approaching King.

SCENE 3

In the Count's palace at Rousillon, the King, Countess, Lafeu, and two French lords entered with attendants. The King, reflecting on recent losses, said, "We lost a jewel in her; our esteem for her made us much poorer by her absence. But your son, mad in folly, lacked the sense to understand her true worth."

The Countess, with a heavy heart, replied, "It's in the past, my liege, and I beg you to see it as the natural rebellion of youth, when passion overpowers reason and burns uncontrollably."

. . .

The King, reassuring her, said, "My honored lady, I have forgiven and forgotten all, though at one time my anger was set high against him, ready to strike."

Lafeu added, "I must say, though I ask pardon first, that the young lord greatly wronged his majesty, his mother, and his lady. But he wronged himself most of all, losing a wife whose beauty amazed even the richest eyes, whose words captivated all ears, and whose perfection made even the proudest hearts humble themselves before her."

The King, reflecting on lost things, said, "Praising what is lost makes the memory dearer. Well, call him here; we are reconciled, and seeing him again will put an end to the past. Let him not ask for our pardon, for his great offense is dead, buried deeper than oblivion. Let him approach as a stranger, not as an offender; inform him that it is our will."

A gentleman left to fetch Bertram. The King then turned to Lafeu and asked, "What does he say about your daughter? Have you spoken with him?"

Lafeu replied, "All that he is now depends on your highness."

. . .

The King, feeling hopeful, said, "Then we shall have a match. I have received letters that praise him highly."

As Bertram entered, Lafeu commented, "He looks well."

The King, addressing Bertram, said, "I am not in a settled mood, for you may see both sunshine and hail in me at once. But just as dark clouds give way to brighter beams, so stand forth; the time is fair again."

Bertram, with remorse, said, "My deeply regretted faults, dear sovereign, I beg your pardon."

The King responded, "All is forgiven; not another word about the past. Let's seize the present moment, for time steals away silently before we can act. Do you remember this lord's daughter?"

Bertram, recalling his first impression, said, "Admiringly, my liege, at first I chose her before my heart dared speak. But then, clouded by scorn, I saw only flaws in her and dismissed her beauty as stolen. I now realize that she whom everyone praised, and whom I have loved since losing her, seemed to me then like dust that offended my eyes."

The King, acknowledging his excuse, said, "Well excused: the fact that you loved her erases much of your offense. But love that comes too late is like a pardon that arrives too slowly, turning what was good into a bitter memory. We often undervalue what we have until it's gone, and our misplaced anger destroys our friends, leaving us to mourn. Let this be Helen's farewell, and forget her. Now, send your affections to fair Maudlin; the necessary consents are in place, and we'll wait here to see your second marriage."

The Countess, praying for a better outcome, said, "May this union be more blessed than the first, or else, heaven, take me before they meet!"

Lafeu urged Bertram, "Come, my son, in whom my house's name must continue, give a token of affection to inspire my daughter."

. . .

Bertram handed over a ring, and Lafeu, examining it, said, "By my old beard, I saw this very ring on Helen's finger at court. It was hers."

Bertram denied it, "It was not hers."

The King, recognizing the ring, asked to see it and said, "This ring was mine; I gave it to Helen and told her that if she ever needed help, she could use this ring as a token to receive it from me. Did you somehow take it from her?"

Bertram, insisting, said, "My gracious sovereign, however you interpret it, the ring was never hers."

The Countess, shocked, exclaimed, "Son, I have seen her wear it, and she valued it more than her life."

Lafeu added, "I am sure I saw her wear it."

Bertram, stubbornly, replied, "You are mistaken, my lord; she never saw this ring. It was thrown to me from a window in

Florence, wrapped in a paper with the name of the noblewoman who threw it. But when I explained I couldn't reciprocate her feelings, she was deeply saddened and refused to take the ring back."

The King, growing suspicious, said, "Plutus himself, the god of wealth, knows no more about alchemy than I do about this ring. It was mine, given to Helen. So, if you know yourself, confess that it was hers and explain how you got it. She swore to the saints that she would never part with it unless she gave it to you in bed, where you have never been, or sent it to us in a time of great need."

Bertram, doubling down, said, "She never saw it."

The King, angered, said, "You speak falsely, as I value my honor. You're raising doubts in me that I'd rather not entertain. If it should prove that you are so inhuman—but it cannot be so—and yet, I don't know: you hated her deeply, and she is dead. Only closing her eyes myself could convince me of her death more than seeing this ring. Take him away."

. . .

As guards seized Bertram, the King continued, "My previous trust in you, regardless of the outcome, now seems misplaced, as I feared too little. Away with him! We'll investigate this matter further."

Bertram, desperate, said, "If you prove that this ring was ever hers, then you can just as easily prove that I was with her in Florence, where she never was."

As Bertram was led away, the King said, "I am wrapped in dark thoughts."

A gentleman entered with a message, "Gracious sovereign, whether I'm to blame or not, I don't know, but here's a petition from a Florentine woman who has been trying to deliver it herself but couldn't reach you. I took it from her, persuaded by her grace and speech. She is here now, waiting to present her case to you."

The King read the petition, "Upon his many promises to marry me when his wife was dead, I blush to say it, he won me. Now the Count Rousillon is a widower: his vows are owed to me, and I have given him my honor. He fled Florence without a word, and I have followed him here to seek justice. Grant it to me, O king! Only you can, or else a seducer will flourish, and a poor maid will be ruined. DIANA CAPILET."

Lafeu, frustrated, declared, "I'll buy a son-in-law at a fair, but I want nothing to do with this one."

The King, seeing the truth unfold, said, "The heavens have brought this to light, Lafeu. Seek out these suitors; bring the count back quickly. I fear Helen's life was taken unfairly."

As Bertram was brought back, the King, still puzzled, asked, "I wonder, sir, since you seem to hate wives so much, why do you desire to marry?"

Just then, the Widow and Diana entered, and the King asked, "Who are these women?"

Diana stepped forward, "I am, my lord, a wretched Florentine from the ancient Capilet family. You know my case, and so you must know how much pity I deserve."

. . .

The Widow added, "I am her mother, sir, and both my age and honor suffer under this complaint we bring, and both shall end unless you provide a remedy."

The King turned to Bertram, "Come here, count; do you know these women?"

Bertram, reluctantly admitted, "My lord, I cannot deny that I know them. Do they accuse me of anything more?"

Diana, challenging him, asked, "Why do you look so strangely at your wife?"

Bertram, denying the accusation, said, "She's not my wife, my lord."

Diana, holding firm, replied, "If you shall marry, you must give away this hand, which is mine, and all the vows you made, which are mine. I am so bound to you by vow that whoever marries you must marry me, either both of us or none."

. . .

Lafeu, seeing through Bertram, said, "Your reputation falls short for my daughter; you're no husband for her."

Bertram, dismissing Diana, said, "My lord, this is a desperate woman whom I've laughed with before. Please believe that I wouldn't lower my honor in such a way."

The King, not yet convinced, replied, "Your deeds must prove your honor, not just your words."

Diana, persisting, said, "My lord, ask him under oath if he does not believe he took my virginity."

The King asked, "What do you say to that?"

Bertram, trying to discredit her, replied, "She's shameless, my lord, and was a common flirt in the camp."

Diana, defending herself, said, "He wrongs me, my lord. If I were so, he could have

. . .

bought me at a common price. Do not believe him. Look at this ring, which was once held in the highest regard and yet, he gave it to a so-called commoner like me, if that's what I am."

The Countess, recognizing the ring, exclaimed, "He's blushing, and that's proof enough. That gem has been in our family for generations, passed down to the next in line. This is his wife; that ring is undeniable proof."

The King, recalling Diana's earlier claim, asked, "Didn't you say there was someone here who could testify?"

Diana, hesitant, said, "I did, my lord, but I'm reluctant to bring forward such a bad witness. His name is Parolles."

Lafeu, recognizing the name, said, "I saw him today, if you can call him a man."

The King ordered, "Find him and bring him here."

. . .

As an attendant left to fetch Parolles, Bertram, worried, asked, "What about him? He's known as a treacherous liar, tainted by every vice in the world. Am I or this lady to be judged by what he says, knowing he'll say anything?"

The King, focusing on the ring, said, "She has your ring."

Bertram, reluctantly admitted, "I believe she does. I liked her and pursued her in my youthful folly. She played hard to get, which only increased my desire, as obstacles often do in matters of love. Eventually, her cunning and charm won me over; she got the ring, and I received what any lesser man could have bought at a market price."

Diana, with patience, said, "I must endure this. You, who cast aside a noble first wife, may treat me just as poorly. But since you lack virtue, I'll lose a husband. Send for your ring; I'll return it, and you can give me mine back."

Bertram, in denial, said, "I don't have it."

The King asked Diana, "What ring was yours, I pray you?"

. . .

Diana, describing it, said, "It's much like the one on your finger."

The King, showing Bertram's ring, said, "Do you recognize this ring? It was his recently."

Diana, confirming, said, "And this is the one I gave him, while in bed."

The King, piecing the story together, said, "But the story you told was that you threw it to him out of a window."

Diana, standing by her truth, said, "I have spoken the truth."

At that moment, Parolles entered, and Bertram, knowing he was caught, confessed, "My lord, I do admit the ring was hers."

. . .

The King, seeing through Bertram's deceit, said, "You falter with every word. Is this the man you spoke of?"

Diana confirmed, "Yes, my lord."

The King, addressing Parolles, said, "Tell me, sir, but tell me truthfully, not fearing your master's displeasure, which I'll protect you from. What do you know of this man and this woman?"

Parolles, trying to be diplomatic, said, "So please your majesty, my master has been an honorable gentleman. He's had his flaws, as gentlemen do."

The King, pressing for the truth, said, "Come, come, get to the point. Did he love this woman?"

Parolles, playing both sides, said, "Faith, sir, he did love her; but how?"

The King, growing impatient, asked, "How, I pray you?"

. . .

Parolles, equivocating, said, "He loved her, sir, as a gentleman loves a woman."

The King, sensing his evasiveness, asked, "And how is that?"

Parolles, offering nothing concrete, replied, "He loved her, sir, and loved her not."

The King, frustrated by Parolles' double talk, said, "You're as much a knave as you are not. What a slippery character you are!"

Parolles, sensing danger, said, "I'm a poor man at your majesty's command."

Lafeu, interjecting, said, "He's a good drummer, my lord, but a poor speaker."

. . .

Diana, adding to the charges, asked, "Do you know he promised me marriage?"

Parolles, evasive again, said, "Faith, I know more than I'll say."

The King, demanding the truth, asked, "But will you not speak all you know?"

Parolles, trying to cover his tracks, said, "Yes, so please your majesty. I did go between them, as I said; but more than that, he loved her. He was mad for her, talking of all sorts of things, and I was so trusted by them that I knew of their going to bed and other matters, like promises of marriage. But I'll say no more, for it would bring me ill will."

The King, seeing through his ploy, said, "You've already said enough, unless you can prove they are married. But you're too clever with your testimony; stand aside."

Turning to Diana, the King asked, "This ring, you say, was yours?"

. . .

Diana confirmed, "Yes, my good lord."

The King, questioning her, asked, "Where did you buy it? Or who gave it to you?"

Diana, straightforwardly, said, "It wasn't given to me, nor did I buy it."

The King, puzzled, asked, "Who lent it to you?"

Diana, again, replied, "It wasn't lent to me either."

The King, still confused, asked, "Then where did you find it?"

Diana, firmly, said, "I didn't find it."

The King, now exasperated, asked, "If it wasn't yours by any of these means, how could you have given it to him?"

. . .

Diana, holding her ground, said, "I never gave it to him."

Lafeu, trying to make sense of it, remarked, "This woman is as changeable as a glove, my lord; she fits and removes herself at will."

The King, recognizing the ring, said, "This ring was mine; I gave it to his first wife."

Diana, not backing down, said, "It might have been yours or hers, for all I know."

The King, growing suspicious, said, "Take her away; I don't like her story. To prison with her and him too. Unless you tell me where you got this ring, you'll die within the hour."

Diana, defiantly, said, "I'll never tell you."

The King, firm in his command, said, "Take her away."

. . .

Diana, offering a solution, said, "I'll provide bail, my liege."

The King, losing patience, said, "I think you're just a common trickster."

Diana, boldly, replied, "By Jove, if I've ever known a man, it was you."

The King, perplexed, asked, "Then why have you accused him all this time?"

Diana, explaining her position, said, "Because he's both guilty and not guilty. He knows I'm not a virgin, and he'll swear to it; I'll swear I am, and he knows nothing. Great king, I'm no harlot, by my life. I'm either a maid or this old man's wife."

The King, tired of the games, said, "She's abusing our ears: take her to prison."

. . .

Diana, before being taken away, called out to her mother, "Good mother, fetch my bail. Stay, royal sir."

The Widow exited, and Diana continued, "The jeweler who owns the ring has been sent for, and he'll vouch for me. As for this lord, who has wronged me as he knows, though he never physically harmed me, I release him. He knows he defiled his wife's bed, and at that time, she was already pregnant. Dead though she may be, she feels her child kick. So, here's my riddle: one who's dead is alive. And now, behold the meaning."

The Widow re-entered, bringing in Helena, alive and well.

The King, astonished, exclaimed, "Is there no illusionist here deceiving my eyes? Is what I see real?"

Helena, addressing the King, said, "No, my good lord; it's just the shadow of a wife you see, the name but not the substance."

. . .

Bertram, overwhelmed, said, "Both, both. O, forgive me!"

Helena, revealing all, said, "O my good lord, when I was like this maid, you were wonderfully kind to me. Here is your ring, and here's your letter; it says, 'When from my finger you can get this ring and are by me with child,' etc. This has been done. Will you be mine, now that you are doubly won?"

Bertram, accepting his fate, said, "If she, my liege, can prove this clearly, I'll love her dearly, forever and ever."

Helena, with confidence, said, "If it doesn't prove true, let a deadly divorce separate us. O, my dear mother, do I see you alive?"

Lafeu, tearing up, said, "My eyes are watering; I'll be crying soon. Good Tom Drum, hand me a handkerchief. Thank you. Come home with me, I'll find some amusement in your company. Let your courtesies be; they are not worth much."

The King, seeking clarity, said, "Let us hear the

. . .

whole story, point by point, to ensure the truth brings pleasure. If you're still a fresh, untouched flower, Diana, choose your husband, and I'll pay your dowry. For I can guess that by your honest aid, you've kept yourself pure, and yet acted as a wife. More details of this story will be told later. Everything seems well, and if it ends so, the bitter past will make the sweet present more welcome."

As they exited with a flourish, the King turned to the audience, delivering the epilogue, "The king's a beggar, now the play is done: All is well ended, if this suit be won, That you express content; which we will pay, With strife to please you, day exceeding day: Ours be your patience then, and yours our parts; Your gentle hands lend us, and take our hearts."

THE END

THE INTRICACIES AND DILEMMAS OF "ALL'S WELL THAT ENDS WELL"

A Tale of Ambition and Virtue: "All's Well That Ends Well" is one of Shakespeare's more complex and less conventional comedies, believed to have been written between 1604 and 1605. The play unfolds across the courts of France and the rural landscapes of Roussillon, weaving a narrative that explores themes of ambition, social mobility, and the often challenging pursuit of love. Imagine a world where the desire to overcome obstacles is met with the unpredictability of human emotions, resulting in a story rich with moral ambiguity and dramatic irony.

The Challenges of Social Hierarchy: At the heart of "All's Well That Ends Well" lies the tension between different social classes. Helena, the daughter of a deceased physician, aims to elevate her status through marriage to Bertram, a nobleman of higher rank. Shakespeare uses this theme to examine the fluidity of social mobility and the challenges that arise when personal ambition intersects with societal expectations. The play questions the traditional boundaries of class and love, making it a unique commentary on the social dynamics of the time.

The Power of Determination: Central to the narrative is Helena's relentless pursuit of her goals, which drives the play forward. Her cleverness and resourcefulness are highlighted as she navigates a world that often underestimates her due to her lower social standing. Helena's journey underscores the themes of perseverance and the belief that virtue and intelligence can overcome societal limitations, offering a narrative that empowers characters traditionally seen as underdogs.

Themes of Deception and Truth: "All's Well That Ends Well" thrives on the tension between deception and truth. Helena's use of a bed trick—where she takes the place of another woman to fulfill Bertram's conditions for marriage—serves as a pivotal plot device that explores the ethics of deception in the pursuit of a righteous end. The play delves into the complexities of honesty, manipulation, and the fine line between achieving one's desires and maintaining moral integrity.

The Role of Gender and Power: The play also examines the dynamics of gender and power, particularly through Helena's unconventional role as a woman who takes control of her own destiny. Shakespeare challenges the traditional passive role of women in romantic pursuits, presenting Helena as a character who actively shapes her future. This exploration of gender roles adds depth to the play's examination of power and agency.

Influence on Literature and Culture: Despite being one of Shakespeare's "problem plays," "All's Well That Ends Well" has influenced literature and culture, particularly in its exploration of themes like social mobility, ambition, and the complexity of human relationships. Its depiction of a strong female protagonist and its nuanced treatment of moral dilemmas continue to resonate, making it a play of enduring relevance.

The Setting of France and Roussillon: The contrasting settings of the sophisticated French court and the more pastoral Roussillon highlight the play's themes of social contrast and the journey between different worlds. These environments frame the characters' struggles and underscore the play's exploration of the clash between individual desires and societal expectations.

The Intersection of Nature and Human Desire: While "All's Well That Ends Well" does not focus heavily on the natural world, it uses the metaphor of "natural" desires versus societal constraints to explore the characters' motivations. The play's title suggests a resolution that aligns with the natural order, yet the journey to this end is fraught with challenges that question the harmony between nature and human ambition.

Shakespeare's Language: The language of "All's Well That Ends Well" is marked by its wit, eloquence, and sometimes biting irony. Shakespeare's use of dialogue to convey the characters' inner conflicts and societal pressures adds depth to the narrative, engaging the audience in the play's exploration of complex themes.

A Story of Resolution and Uncertainty: "All's Well That Ends Well" concludes with a resolution that, while seemingly happy, leaves lingering questions about the nature of love, truth, and fulfillment. The play invites audiences to reflect on the consequences of ambition, the ethics of deception, and the possibility of genuine happiness within the constraints of societal norms. It remains a thought-provoking and intricately woven masterpiece that challenges conventional notions of comedy and resolution.

THE LIFE OF WILLIAM SHAKESPEARE

Step back in time with us as we discover the exciting life of **William Shakespeare**—a storyteller whose magnificent tales have been told and retold for hundreds of years. Fasten your seatbelts for some amazing facts about the Bard of Avon!

Birthday Mystery: Believe it or not, we don't know exactly when Shakespeare was born. Historians guess it was around April 23, 1564, but that's all because of the date of his baptism. How curious that such a famous person has a birthday shrouded in mystery!

. . .

School Days: Young Shakespeare attended the King's New School in his hometown, where he learned important subjects like Latin, Greek, history, and poetry—all without the gadgets and technology students have today.

Word Wizard: Shakespeare had a way with words, inventing over 1,700 of them! Imagine, every time you say "bedroom" or "excitement," you're using words that Shakespeare introduced to the English language.

Globe Trotter - But Not Really: The Globe Theatre is where Shakespeare's masterpieces were first performed—not a globe you can spin, but a large, round, open-air theater where audiences marveled under the sky.

Super-sized Works: Our dear Bard wrote 37 plays and 154 sonnets. That's a lot of storytelling! If you wrote a poem every week of the year, you'd still be short of Shakespeare's sonnet count.

Nicknamed "The Bard": Shakespeare is often referred to as "The Bard of Avon." 'Bard' means poet, and indeed, Shakespeare was a master poet from the town of Stratford-upon-Avon.

Lovey-Dovey Lines: Shakespeare's words about love are so beautiful that they are still read at weddings and shared between sweethearts today. And if you've heard the phrase "to be or not to be," you're quoting one of his most famous lines!

Queen for a Fan: Queen Elizabeth I loved the theater, and Shakespeare's plays were some of her most enjoyed performances. It was quite the honor for Shakespeare to entertain her majesty with his work.

Shakespeare's Secret Code: Some folks believe that Shakespeare tucked away secret codes within his plays—making each performance not just a show, but also a puzzle full of hidden meanings.

Goodnight, Sweet Prince: At age 52, in the year 1616, Shakespeare took his final bow. His presence may be missed, but his stories live on, continuing to inspire, entertain, and provoke thought across the globe.

. . .

So there you have it—a little peek into the life of the man who has kept us company through his words for over four centuries. Open the pages of his stories, and let William Shakespeare's plays transport you to a world where imagination knows no bounds. Happy reading!

It's hard for books to get noticed these days. Whether you liked this one or not, please consider writing a review, thanks!

Jeanette Vigon

SHAKESPEARE FOR KIDS - OTHER BOOKS IN THE SERIES

SHAKESPEARE FOR KIDS - OTHER BOOKS IN THE SERIES

- Much Ado About Nothing
- The Comedy of Errors
- As You Like It
- The Merchant of Venice
- The Tempest
- King Lear
- A Midsummer Night's Dream
- Julius Caesar
- Hamlet

SHAKESPEARE FOR KIDS - OTHER BOOKS IN THE SERIES

You can find the rest of the books in the series here:

https://amzn.to/3wLXpTC

Made in the USA
Columbia, SC
16 May 2025